What
Are You
Grateful
For?

SWEET GRATITUDE

A New World of
Raw Desserts

Matthew Rogers
AND
Tiziana Alipo Tamborra

Foreword by
Terces Engelhart

North Atlantic Books
Berkeley, California

Published by
North Atlantic Books
P.O. Box 12327
Berkeley, California 94712

Cover photos © Jamie Soja
Interior photos courtesy of Jamie Soja, Anthony Mendez, and Jack Huynh
Cover and book design © Ayelet Maida, A/M Studios
Printed in the United States of America

Sweet Gratitude: A New World of Raw Desserts is sponsored by the Society for the Study of Native Arts and Sciences, a nonprofit educational corporation whose goals are to develop an educational and cross-cultural perspective linking various scientific, social, and artistic fields; to nurture a holistic view of arts, sciences, humanities, and healing; and to publish and distribute literature on the relationship of mind, body, and nature.

North Atlantic Books' publications are available through most bookstores. For further information, visit our Web site at www.northatlanticbooks.com or call 800-733-3000.

Library of Congress Cataloging-in-Publication Data
Rogers, Matthew, cook.
    Sweet gratitude : a new world of raw desserts / Matthew Rogers and Tiziana Alipo Tamborra ; foreword by Terces Engelhart.
        p. cm.
    Includes index.
    Summary: "An inspirational cookbook that explores the cutting-edge culinary world of raw desserts and offers exotic, gourmet, original recipes for cakes, pies, cheesecake, parfaits, cookies, and chocolates for anyone looking for healthy yet delicious and decadent sweets"—Provided by publisher.
    ISBN 978-1-55643-744-1
    1. Desserts. 2. Raw foods. 3. Café Gratitude (Restaurant) I. Tamborra, Tiziana Alipo. II. Title.
    TX773.R644 2008
    641.8'6—dc22
                                                2008015753

3 4 5 6 7 8 9 UNITED 14 13 12 11 10 09

This book is dedicated
with Love,
to our mothers,

Maria Marega

and

Yolanda Rogers

Contents

Acknowledgments

We would first like to express our deepest gratitude to Matthew and Terces Engelhart for making this book possible. They are the ones who inspired our collaboration and this project. We want to acknowledge them for fully trusting us and for constantly encouraging our passion for and commitment to the development of these unique desserts; for the unconditional support they have given us throughout the completion of this book; for sharing their knowledge and experience so generously; and for standing for vibrant health and personal transformation.

We want to thank the Bakery team of Café Gratitude, past and present, as every baker has contributed to the testing and refining of many of these recipes and inspiring the creation of new ones. Thank you Zoi Hall, Arielle Webb, Estevan Sifuentes, Simone Power, Sarah Stevens, Daniel Korson, Charlie Ward, Judea Johnson, Eden Rumelt, Daphne Saliba, Tom Gibson, Kendra Presley, Katrina Vaillancourt, Leif Mendias, Caitlin Browning, Treasure Van Dinther, Orchid, Stephanie Sue Brendle, Vicky Zettler, Chad Johnston, Natasha Underwood, Jill, Chaya Diehl, Lyn, Mandy, Todd Haack, K Lemasters, Deb Lewis, Carmen Vasquez.

We are grateful to all Café Gratitude managers for the sharing and guidance they have provided us and their hard work and commitment; all Café Gratitude employees for sharing our visions and their constant appreciation of our creations; and a special thank you goes out to the Central Kitchen employees for providing us, on a daily basis, with all the basic ingredients that make our creations possible. We truly are blessed to be part of such an incredible community.

We want to thank Elaina Love and David Wolfe for their outstanding contribution to raw food and for being an inspiration for learning, developing, and mastering new ideas.

We are thankful for all our vendors, especially Transition Nutrition, Essential Living Food, HealthForce Nutritionals, Organic Planet, and Premier Organics.

Thank you to photographer Jamie Soja for all of the dessert photos and cover picture and to photographers Anthony Mendez and Jack Huynh for their beautiful contribution.

Thank you to Linda and all the team at Spun Sugar bakery supply for always sharing so openly their valuable knowledge and tips for the making of many wedding cakes.

We want to acknowledge all our friends and families for being so generous and patient during the creation of this project and for sharing their ideas, feedback, and constructive opinions.

Thank you Trixxie Carr for all your inspiring input, and to Daniel Korson for your valuable contribution to the chocolate world. A special thanks goes to Anthony Mendez and Henry DeFauw for their unconditional love and support.

Finally we want to acknowledge and thank the teachers, health enthusiasts, leaders, practitioners, pastry chefs, and the people who have touched and inspired us in the search for new ways of living a healthy and sweet life. Thank you all!

Foreword

When Matthew and Tiziana first came to us saying they would love the opportunity to create a recipe book of the desserts from Café Gratitude, we were inspired. Not only have they created the most amazing selection of live-vegan desserts ever, they have done so in the context of Café Gratitude's mission, keeping their attention on all they have to be grateful for. That's not always as easy as it may seem. Life presents us with many challenges, and they have had theirs, but always they've come through to the other side with an expanded capacity to love and be loved.

Matthew has taken on his passion for raw chocolate and gifted the world with a variety of truffles, fudge, and dipped chocolates, while Tiziana has given birth to the most beautiful live-vegan wedding cakes. Their mutual love of celebrating life comes through in their ingenious creations. They have now partnered their talents and this book is the result. As you look through these pages you can see what is possible when we surrender to being of service to others, to making a difference, and to trusting the process of opening up to love.

I couldn't be prouder of these two beings. I know that their contribution will be joyously received and appreciated. Not only are their desserts delicious, beautiful, and creative, they are filled with love, which also makes them healing.

With deep gratitude and love,
Terces Engelhart
Owner of Café Gratitude

Introduction

Sweet Gratitude uniquely merges a "cookbook" of delicious raw vegan desserts with the philosophy of celebrating life and love for ourselves, each other, and the world. We want to inspire people to become aware of their own power in the choices they make and to understand the infinite effects that these choices have. Being present to every choice we make is a way to honor and celebrate our lives, our bodies, and the Earth. Choosing vegan, organic, and fair-trade foods has a major impact on the planet and all the beings nourished and supported by this planet.

Taking responsibility for how we nourish ourselves goes beyond our food choices. We nourish ourselves with our thoughts, the way we express ourselves, and how present we are in the moment. Throughout the book we will be sharing our thoughts and experiences with concepts such as love, trust, forgiveness, freedom, and self-worth. All this is connected with our everyday lives, our experiences, and the oneness of the world.

Why raw desserts? Well, for many reasons, but perhaps primarily because they are one of the healthiest dessert choices available. These desserts are the most delicious, most vibrantly pure and beautiful desserts one can eat. Desserts in the raw are ideally done with fruit in its ripe, organic, bursting-with-flavor wholeness. Most of the ingredients used are fresh and minimally processed, in their natural nutrient-rich state. Miracles then occur as these raw ingredients are blended, strained, soaked, frozen, dehydrated, or whipped into delicious pies, cakes, candies, or ice cream. The possibilities are endless with what can be created and re-created combining these techniques with a wide variety of ingredients.

We use alternative sweeteners such as agave syrup, dates, and yacon syrup—they are natural, lower on the glycemic index, and delicious. Many of the desserts we include here are raw versions of long-time familiar favorites, while others feature more exotic, sophisticated flavors and textures that are not widely experienced. All are divinely decadent, with a simplicity and elegance in their wholesomeness that only Mother Nature could provide. Raw desserts and raw food in general are real foods, food the body understands and is nourished by.

For many people, these are the safest kinds of desserts to eat. Those who are lactose-intolerant, borderline diabetic, or allergic to wheat gluten find raw desserts to be a godsend. People with these conditions are increasing in number as our bodies react to all the processed high-glycemic sugar, wheat, and pasteurized dairy that

Anything is possible! Raw wedding cakes

is ubiquitous in today's modern world. Those who are dieting and/or have high cholesterol can profoundly benefit from switching over to raw desserts. For some people who are moving through a healing time, these desserts might be the only kind of sweets their bodies can handle. Vegans, vegetarians, and all people who just love organic, good food absolutely adore raw desserts. One may choose raw desserts for any of these reasons, but they really are for everybody to enjoy. People are completely amazed that you can have desserts this good without any animal products or cooking. What's far more amazing is that many of these recipes undeniably taste more decadent and flavorful than the "real thing"!

A Few Personal Words from Tiziana

I've always been fascinated with all expressions of cooking, but desserts in particular have a special place in my heart. My passion for desserts is one of the greatest gifts I've received from my mother and grandmother. As far back as I can remember, I was their precious assistant. My fondest memories are watching and assisting them with big baking and cooking projects. I can still remember all the preparation and anticipation, the making of something unique using different techniques and flavors, the feeling of collaboration and complicity. Some of those specialties were made only once a year, and I always looked forward to those celebrations with trepidation and excitement. Christmas was my favorite—we would bake overnight and prepare the most unique desserts. Those desserts would later become our gifts for family members and friends, and our treats for the holidays.

In the early '90s I was exposed to macrobiotic cooking and philosophy, and for the first time I realized that another way of creating desserts was possible. I was so inspired by the concept of creating delicious desserts that were also healthy that I immediately started to transform the recipes I knew into vegan, macrobiotic versions. Desserts were my key to the gate of healthy foods and nutrition. I continued to study macrobiotics in Italy, and I knew in my heart that desserts and health were going to be on my path, in whatever manifestation and direction it would take me.

I provided the local farmer's market with my own creations for several years, and I was amazed by how well they were received and how much gratitude I experienced from my community. To further my knowledge in nutrition, I came to the U.S. in 1997, where I continued my studies at the Vega Study Center in California with macrobiotic pioneers Herman and Cornelia Aihara and teachers David and Cynthia Briscoe. Over the following years I baked for several international macrobiotic conferences and cruises, worked as a private chef and a pastry chef, taught cooking classes, and managed two vegan bakeries.

In 2005 I first met Matthew and Terces Engelhart, owners of Café Gratitude. I was just looking for a job, really, and I knew nothing about raw desserts. In fact, I was totally skeptical and had no idea what to expect! I was truly blown away to discover what is possible with the variety and versatility of so many new ingredients, and how good and flavorful these desserts are. A new world of possibilities opened before my eyes, and the journey continues. The transition from baked to raw desserts was easier than I expected. I joyfully embraced the challenge and was immediately inspired to apply my previous baking experiences to the discovery of new styles of raw desserts. I've fully devoted myself to mastering the most harmonious flavors and presentations, sharing my experience and love for desserts, and creating many new recipes while continuing to improve old ones.

A year later I made my first raw wedding cake, and many more have followed since. I am currently the Bakery Manager for the Café and continually embrace the never-ending possibilities of desserts, as well as my own personal transformation.

This book is the fruit of all my passion, my love for sweetness, and my commitment to share and inspire anybody to enjoy delicious, healthy desserts. I'm honored and touched that I've been given the chance to bring sweetness into many people's lives!

A Few Personal Words from Matthew

One of my earliest memories is of being in the sandbox playing the "baker." I made cakes, pies, and cookies out of the available materials of mud, sand, and rocks. I remember having so much fun building these sometimes-elaborate creations, especially when presenting the finished product to people for their "enjoyment." The gift of giving has throughout my life provided me with the most fulfillment. There is nothing that makes me happier than the act of creating something and giving it away for someone else's enjoyment.

I am aware of the many talents I have been blessed with in this life, and working with food is certainly up at the top. I was so interested in food as a profession that when I was twenty I trained as a pastry chef. That only lasted a year, and I left the school rather disillusioned with the restaurant industry and especially with all the unhealthy things we were preparing. I would have never guessed back then that the universe really did want me to work with food! My path to where I am today has unfolded in front of my eyes, and I've just had to go along with it.

After living on an organic permaculture farm in Maui called Lau Lima, which is owned by Café Gratitude founders Matthew and Terces Engelhart, I moved to San Francisco and got my first over-the-table job in seven years at the Café. I was immediately drawn into the dessert world and soon became the main dessert chef for the company. Raw desserts came very naturally, much more like making mud and sand pies than the stuff I made in culinary school. I reworked and refined some of Terces' recipes and started inventing many others. The happiness I experienced was profound, for not only was I getting to create delicious and beautiful desserts, these totally cutting-edge desserts were raw, vegan, organic, and actually healthy for people! Over time I mastered the art of raw desserts, constantly created new items, started teaching classes on the subject, and now here is the fruit of my labors: a book. This book is probably the greatest gift I've ever given. I am honored, blessed, and ecstatically joyful to give this book to the world to enjoy.

We Are Grateful

We would like to acknowledge all the customers, employees, and community of Café Gratitude for making this book possible. Without their feedback, ecstatic love for our creations, nurturing positive support, and appreciation we would have never taken raw desserts this far. We really stepped into the unknown with raw desserts and discovered a huge, beautiful world! Part of our vision for this book is to inspire people to embrace and connect with what might be different or unknown. Taking a chance, whether or not it involves food, is where we really get to taste all the adventure, magic, and mystery in life.

We also would like to thank the reader for taking a chance! Thank you for your commitment to your own health and that of your loved ones. Thank you for honoring the Earth. Thank you for contributing to the new paradigm of food consciousness: Raw!

CHAPTER 1

Ingredient Preparation, Equipment, and Resources

The Power of Choice

All of us are blessed with the power of choice at any given moment. Even when there are circumstances that we have no control over, we still have the power to choose who we will be and how we will act in the face of that circumstance. The power of choice is basically the same concept as free will. This is one of our greatest gifts as humans. We create our own experience through our thoughts, speech, beliefs, actions, and attitudes. We choose, either consciously or unconsciously, all of these things in every moment. We are never powerless unless we choose so.

Our choices are not isolated incidents, they are powerful decisions that create a ripple effect on the rest of the world. What we choose now sooner or later has a direct impact, not just on ourselves, but on many others and the whole planet. Sometimes what we choose is influenced by habit or by what makes us comfortable. To step into our power of choice is to be consciously aware of why we are making a choice and to be present to its impact.

It is important to carefully choose the proper equipment and the best ingredients to have good results with these recipes. Choosing ingredients that are seasonal, fresh, organic, and local will greatly affect the end result, regardless of which desserts you choose to make. For specialty ingredients that are available year-round such as nuts, cacao, and oils, we suggest choosing the highest quality available. We are all worth it!

In this chapter we give directions for preparing the basic ingredients that will be used throughout the book. This includes how to make all the nut milks and flours, coconut milk, date paste, and anything that requires specific preparation in order to be used in the recipe. We also list the necessary equipment and tools for the proper and successful making of the desserts. A list of resources at the end of the chapter will help you find specialty ingredients not commonly available. The most important aspect of ingredient preparation is choosing the best ingredients available. In general, whatever recipe you choose to make, please read through the entire recipe in advance so you can have a sense of all the ingredients and steps involved.

For preparation of Irish moss, see Chapter 8, page 182.

Useful Tips for Selecting and Storing Nuts

Special attention should always be given when selecting nuts. All nuts, if improperly stored, will become stale or rancid. The higher the oil content in the nut, the more easily it will spoil. In general, softer nuts tend to have a higher oil content. For this reason, we recommend always storing macadamia, Brazil, and pecan nuts in the fridge in an airtight container.

Always smell and taste nuts before using, and if possible, before buying; if they are rancid the odor will be a sharp, strong, chemical-like smell. We suggest purchasing nuts in quantities that will be used in a short period of time. All nuts should be stored in an airtight container to ensure freshness for as long as possible.

Making Nut Milk/Nut Flour

You can make nut "milk" out of almost any kind of nut. The process is very simple. All you do is blend soaked or unsoaked (depending on the nut) nuts with water and strain out the milk using a nut-milk bag or something comparable. Nut-milk bags are fine-mesh straining bags with a drawstring, specifically designed for the purpose of

Pouring nut milk through the bag   Straining the nut milk

making nut milk. The pulp left behind after straining is nut "flour," which can be used in a variety of ways. We use nut flour extensively in all our cakes and in some dehydrated items.

Making almond milk requires first soaking the almonds 12–24 hours. After soaking, drain water and rinse the almonds. They are now ready for milk-making.

Hazelnuts and Brazil nuts do not require soaking, as they do not contain the enzyme inhibitors found in most nuts with brown skins.

Add to blender 1 cup nuts and 3 cups filtered water.

Blend on high 2–3 minutes or until nuts are completely broken down. Don't blend too long or the milk will start to overheat. *Optional:* Let nut milks steep 10–20 minutes before straining for a creamier, richer flavor.

Place a nut-milk bag in a bowl or other container. Pour the blended nuts through the nut-milk bag and strain out as much of the milk as possible by firmly squeezing the bag.

Pour milk into a container and store in fridge. Most nut milks will keep for at least three days if stored properly.

Empty the contents (nut flour) of the nut-milk bag. Keep nut flours in an airtight container in the fridge. Nut flour will keep for at least two days. You can store nut flour longer by freezing it.

Nut flour

Soaking Nuts

Soaking Cashews

Soak cashews in cold filtered water for 8 hours (less time is needed if the cashews are broken up into little bits). Soaking them overnight in the fridge is a perfectly fine and easy method for cashews and most other nuts. Once soaked, drain off the water and rinse once or twice. Soaked cashews will keep in the fridge for up to a week, but they require a daily rinsing. Also, make sure they are thoroughly soaked by biting into one and seeing if it has any white in the middle (like pasta). If it does, it needs more soak time. Recipes will specify if a nut is to be soaked; otherwise the nuts being used are always dry.

Soaking and Dehydrating Other Nuts

This is certainly an extra step in preparing ingredients for a crust, but it does make the end result easier to digest. Nuts with enzyme inhibitors include almonds, walnuts, and pecans. Soak the nuts as directed in "Making Nut Milk/Nut Flour," then lay nuts out in a single layer on a dehydrator sheet. Dehydrate at 115° overnight or until the nut is dry and crispy. These nuts are then ready to use in preparing a crust. You can of course skip this step altogether and just use raw nuts as we do in most of these recipes; but soaking them deactivates the enzymes inhibitors.

Preparing Coconut Milk/Meat/Flakes

The first thing you need to do when preparing coconut milk/meat is to open the coconuts.

Start by placing the coconut on its side. With a sharp chef's knife begin to shave the top portion of the husk, exposing the inner shell. Thai young coconuts have a pre-shaved pointed tip on the top, and this is the side you want to shave down.

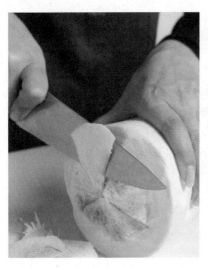 

Shaving the top husk of the coconut   Tapping the coconut shell

Using the square corner of the blade (by the knife's handle), begin tapping the exposed coconut shell, going around in a circle, until you have created a "lid" you can pry open.

Pour the coconut water into a container or directly into the blender. If it appears that there are coconut shell pieces in the water you will want to use a strainer.

With a metal spoon, scrape the inside of the coconut to remove the coconut flesh or "meat."

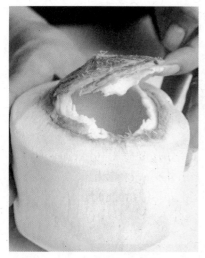  

Prying open the coconut "lid"   Pouring the coconut water   Scooping out the coconut meat

Clean off any small bits of coconut shell and/or brown fibrous skin. You may need to use a peeler for this. Add the cleaned meat to the blender and blend on high until smooth (2–3 minutes). There is your coconut milk!

For recipes that require amounts of coconut meat only, you must open the coconut, drain and set aside the water (use for drinking), and scrape out the meat. Clean the coconut meat and put in a container in the fridge until ready to use. Some recipes may require opening several coconuts.

All coconuts will vary in size, amount of water, and amount of meat inside. This makes coconut milk a huge variable in these recipes. As a general guideline, if the meat inside the coconut is thicker than a quarter of an inch, don't use quite all the meat as this will make the milk too thick. And vice versa—if the meat inside is thin and like a translucent jelly, don't use all the water as this will make the milk too thin. One Thai young coconut usually yields about 1½ cups of milk. The consistency of the coconut milk we use in these recipes is fairly thick. For the ideal thickness, blend 4 ounces (weight) of coconut meat with 1 cup coconut water.

Coconut flakes are widely available; just make sure they are raw and organic. If you do choose to make your own coconut flakes simply grate the mature, hard coconut meat and dehydrate at 115° for several hours or until dry.

Making Date Paste

The fastest and best way to make date paste is to finely mince pitted dates. You can also paddle the chopped-up dates with a little water in a Kitchen-Aid (don't use too much water—it will dilute the flavor and make the dates too wet). An old-fashioned hand-cranked meat grinder will also work perfectly. Or you can always get out the old mortar and pestle!

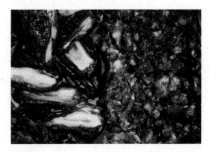

Date paste is available but hard to find. Using paste is really only essential in preparing crusts and in cakes. Regular pitted dates blend up just fine in the blender. Dates are a major variable in these recipes. They range between being really dry and really moist.

Pitted dates and chopped-up date "paste"

When selecting dates choose ones that are not overly dry or overly ripe and squishy. Ten ounces (weight) of date paste is about 1½ cups. We use the widely available Medjool dates in all these recipes.

Melting Oils

All the fat ingredients we use (coconut oil and cacao butter) need to be in their melted oil form when used in the recipes. Simply put the hardened butter in a bowl and place within a larger bowl that has hot water in it. Never melt in a saucepan over an open flame.

Up until recently, the terms coconut "oil" and coconut "butter" were used interchangeably; oil was simply the melted form and butter the hardened form. A new, truly incredible product has been introduced to the market by the nut-butter company Premier Organics, which has now changed the definition of coconut "butter." This coconut butter product is not simply the extracted oil but a combination of virgin coconut oil and creamed, mature coconut meat. It really is more like a butter, such as almond or peanut butter.

Most of our recipes use coconut oil, either in its scented extra-virgin or unscented form. Coconut oil and cacao butter are used in raw desserts to create a firm, creamy, sliceable consistency. Without this ingredient everything would have to be served in a bowl! Unscented coconut oil is extra-virgin oil that has been filtered to minimize its strong coconut aroma and flavor. We mainly use unscented coconut oil as it does not add coconut flavor to the recipes. Individual recipes will specify when to use "extra-virgin coconut oil," "coconut oil," or "coconut butter." Extra-virgin coconut oil is much easier to find than the unscented version, which is mainly available online. You can use the extra-virgin oil anywhere a recipe calls for "coconut oil," just be aware that doing this will add a distinct coconut flavor.

Using Vanilla Bean

All recipes will call for either "liquid vanilla," which is simply whole vanilla beans blended with water, or "vanilla bean," which means using the scraped insides *only* of the vanilla bean. To obtain the precious insides of vanilla beans, you need to slice the bean lengthwise and open it up. With a small spoon, gently scrape out all the black caviar-like vanilla seeds.

Making Liquid Vanilla

To make your own liquid vanilla, take three vanilla beans and chop them up into small pieces. Put in blender and add 1 cup water. Blend for a couple of minutes or until the mixture starts to feel warm and the vanilla beans are completely broken down. Store in an airtight bottle or jar kept in the fridge. Liquid vanilla will last for several weeks, if not longer. You can also create your own ratio of vanilla bean to water to suit your individual taste.

Quick Juicing

"Quick juicing" is our term for the technique of quickly obtaining small quantities of beet and ginger juices. Often only a few tablespoons of these juices are required, and this method is ideal for small quantities. The fastest way to juice these items is to use a proper ginger grater, commonly available in health food stores. You can also employ a regular standing grater, using the side that will produce the smallest grate. Make sure that you have the grater standing over a plate or bowl to collect the juice and grated pulp. (Simply squeeze the juice out of the pulp with your hands.) Collect the juice in a small bowl or measuring cup.

Making Pomegranate Juice

Making fresh, delicious pomegranate juice is much easier and faster than you may expect. Start by slicing the pomegranates horizontally through the middle. Cutting them horizontally is key to having the kernels come out easily. You will need a large bowl and a serving spoon (a metal spoon works best). Hold the halved pomegranate over the bowl with the open side resting on the palm of your hand. Begin firmly tapping the outside of the pomegranate with the spoon. The kernels will start to fall out into your hand. Make sure you are tapping around the entire surface to release all the seeds. When finished, check the bowl for any small white fibrous pieces and remove.

Place all the kernels in a blender. Pulse-blend not more than four to five times. You only want to pulse long enough to pop open the kernels. Over-pulsing will start to blend the kernels and release a tannic, bitter, and astringent flavor. Pour through a nut-milk bag and squeeze out the juice.

Making Cold-Pressed Espresso

Making your own cold-pressed coffee/espresso is fairly easy, healthier than regular brewed coffee, and less wasteful. Specific cold-processing kits in many sizes are available; otherwise you simply use a French press. To make 1 cup of espresso, take ½ cup freshly ground coffee and put in the French press with 1½ cups filtered water. Stir to break apart any chunks and let sit somewhere undisturbed at room temperature for 24–48 hours. For "brewing" larger amounts of cold-pressed coffee, soak 1 pound of coffee with 13 cups water. Remember, good-tasting coffee starts with good-tasting filtered water. Always use a yummy, good-quality, dark-roast coffee for maximum flavor.

Salt

Some salts or particular batches of salt may be too coarse and granular for these recipes. In this case you want to powder the salt using either a coffee grinder or a mortar and pestle. This is most important for recipes in the Cacao chapter, and to be on the safe side always powder salt for those recipes. Salt is extremely important in achieving a balanced flavor. Choose a good-quality, non-refined salt. We only use and highly recommend Himalayan Crystal Salt.

Measuring

It is highly important to measure accurately all ingredients for successful results. The measurements in our recipes are given in cups (volume), ounces (weight), "wet" measurements, or in tablespoons or teaspoons.

Volume measurements in cups are used for all liquids, most of the nuts, coconut oil and flakes, and cacao butter and powder.

Measurements in weight are given in ounces and are used for date paste, Irish moss, cacao powder, fruit, and small amounts of nuts or coconut meat. Measurements for some of these ingredients will also be specified in cups, but we highly recommend using a scale to be 100% accurate.

"Wet" Measurements

You will notice that some recipes specify "wet" measurements for certain ingredients. This means that it is not a liquid ingredient, and thus you want to measure these items combined with the liquid ingredients already in the blender or measuring cup. Do this by adding the solid ingredient to the container holding liquid ingredients, thereby raising the entire liquid volume by the amount specified. For example, when making the Coconut Cream Pie, add to the 2 cups of coconut milk in the blender or measuring cup enough coconut meat to raise the total volume to 2½ cups, for a ½-cup wet measurement of coconut meat.

Measuring ½ cup of coconut meat in a measuring cup by itself is not the same amount; it is actually much less. We occasionally include measurements in this way to have the most consistent end result.

Measuring Equivalents

16 ounces = 1 pound weight
16 cups = 1 gallon
4 cups = 1 quart
2 cups = 1 pint
1 cup = 16 tablespoons
½ cup = 8 tablespoons
⅓ cup = 5 tablespoons + 1 teaspoon
¼ cup = 4 tablespoons
1 tablespoon = 3 teaspoons

Cacao Powder Weight and Volume Equivalents

⅓ cup = 1 ounce weight
½ cup = 1½ ounces weight
⅔ cup = 2 ounces weight
1 cup = 3 ounces weight

Necessary Equipment and Tools

- Food processor (we recommend Cuisinart or Robot-Coupe brands)
- Blender (we recommend Vita-Mix or K-tech brands)
- Mixer (we recommend Kitchen Aid brand)
- Dehydrator (we recommend Excalibur brand)
- Hand-cranked ice cream maker
- Scale (any scale with ounce increments and at least a 16-ounce capacity)
- Measuring cups (cups with ⅓-cup increments and 1-quart capacity are helpful)
- Measuring spoons (stainless-steel spoon sets are best)
- Coffee grinder
- Bowls (large and small)
- Pans (9-inch pie pan, 10-inch cheesecake springform pan, 9-inch cake pan with removable bottom, 8x8x3-inch square pan for Tiramisu or Cobbler)
- Truffle scoop or 1½-inch small ice cream scoop
- Non-stick baking sheet or baking sheet used with wax paper
- Chocolate cup molds or mini-muffin paper baking cups
- Grater, zester, peeler
- Spatulas and spoons (a variety of sizes and styles is helpful)
- Knives (large chef's knife, along with serrated and non-serrated paring knives)
- Piping kit (for decorating)
- Rolling pin

Ingredient Resources

Health food stores and farmers' markets are ideal places for finding fresh, seasonal, local, and organic fruits and nuts. However, many of the ingredients we use are best purchased (or can only be purchased) online for mail delivery. The following websites specialize in raw-food products, equipment, tools, and information:

www.cafegratitude.com
www.purejoyplanet.com
www.essentiallivingfoods.com
www.healthforce.com
www.premierorganics.org
www.eatraw.com
www.rawguru.com
www.chefdepot.com
www.royalhimalayan.com
www.goraw.com
www.excaliburdehydrator.com
www.sunfood.com
www.vitamix.com
www.cuisinart.com
www.kitchenaid.com
www.robotcoupeusa.com
www.omeganutrition.com

CHAPTER 2

Pies

Living in the Present

All we have is this present moment. The past is gone, and the future has not happened yet. Our thoughts are constantly dwelling on the past or projecting into the future. In both instances we are not living in the present moment. This is a natural process in our lives since we are the product of our past and the creators of our future. It is important to not get stuck in either the past or the future because we will not be able to fully experience the magic of the present moment. When we are fully present in the "now" moment we are completely aware of ourselves, our bodies, our surroundings, and the sensations we experience. In the now moment we feel more alive and connected with everything. Communication becomes easier, and our intuition becomes a powerful voice we can trust. Synchronicities start fitting together like puzzle pieces, and we experience the wonder and mystery of life.

Being present is an ongoing daily practice. To get present we must let go of our attachments from the past and our expectations of the future. The first step in letting go of our past is for us to be willing to heal and fully accept what was. We can't change our past, but we can change how we relate to it. When we are creating our future we must be willing to accept different possibilities than the ones we desire. It is important to be engaged in the constructive planning of our future, which we do with our intention, vision, and thoughts. All this planning will simply remain intention, vision, and thoughts unless we take action in the present moment. As we take action in the now to realize our visions, we must stay present and be open to new possibilities of how our visions will manifest.

Preparing food is a great way to practice living in the present. The best results with any recipe will come about from being focused and attentive to every step of the process. Noticing all the colors, flavors, textures, measurements, and shapes of the ingredients naturally brings us into the present moment. Enjoy living in the moment as you make these delicious pies. We guarantee that the pie won't stay in the present moment for very long!

Many of our pies are raw versions of traditional classics. Others are the result of our own creation, utilizing seasonal fruits and other delicious flavors. All these pies are unique and are probably the most loved of all our desserts. For the crusts we mainly use a combination of nuts, which are simply processed with salt, vanilla, and a little date for sweetening and binding purposes. There are also two nut-free pies included here—the Coconut Cream Pie and Banana Cream Pie. The fillings vary greatly but generally include nut or coconut milks, juices, fresh fruits, Irish moss, cacao, and coconut oil.

Also included in this chapter are our amazing tarts and the incredibly quick and easy-to-prepare Fruit Cobbler. Most of these recipes are fairly easy to make and to serve, since the assembling directions are minimal. We can assure you that there is at least one pie here that will become your new favorite!

Recipes

Equipment Needed

- Blender
- Food processor
- Measuring cups
- Measuring spoons
- Scale
- Spatulas
- Dehydrator (for Apple Pie only)
- 9-inch pie pan

Making the Pie Crust

Pie crust recipes may include:

- Nuts or coconut flakes
- Salt
- Date paste
- Liquid vanilla
- Cacao powder/nibs
- Coconut oil

Please see Chapter 1 for details on preparation of these ingredients.

PIE CRUST DIRECTIONS

1. Add the individual recipe's crust ingredients to the food processor. In recipes that use date paste, include half the amount in this step.
2. Process all ingredients until the crust starts to rise on the sides of the processor bowl. Stop the machine and mix with a spatula or spoon.
3. Repeat a few times until nuts are well broken down. Add remaining date paste (if called for in recipe) and continue processing until mixture is consistent. The final result of the crust should be a mixture that can hold together with a gentle pressure and can be broken apart with a clean break.
4. Lightly grease entire inside of pie pan with some coconut oil. Some nuts become very oily after processing and don't require this step, such as crusts that are entirely macadamia nut.
5. Distribute crust evenly on the bottom and sides of pie pan and lightly compact by hand. Decorate edge of crust to your liking. Crust should rise above the rim of the pan, not more than a half inch. Set aside until ready to be filled.

Crusts made entirely with macadamias can easily be over-processed, making the "dough" very oily and too soft to hold a shape in the pie pan. You want to stop processing and stir often, noticing the progressive change in consistency. If you happen to over-process the macadamias, don't worry—they are not useless. Turn them into Macadamia Caramel (page 127).

If the nuts are too chunky, first try sharpening the "S" blade of your processor. You can also lightly process the nuts and salt before adding other ingredients. Adding all the date paste at once will not allow the nuts to break down properly.

When pressing crust into the pan, be careful not to use too much pressure, as this will result in the crust sticking to the pan and making the serving process challenging. On the other hand, if you are not pressing it enough the crust will be crumbly and messy.

If crust is not sticking together and breaking apart with a clean break, you need to add a small splash (½–1 teaspoon) of liquid vanilla and process a bit longer.

Making the Pie Fillings

The basic ingredients needed for most of the pie fillings are:

- Nut milk, coconut milk, juices, or fresh fruits/vegetables
- Agave syrup
- Pitted dates
- Salt
- Liquid vanilla
- Lecithin
- Coconut oil
- Cacao powder and/or butter
- Any additional ingredient the recipe calls for (such as almond butter, espresso, etc.)

Please see Chapter 1 for details on preparation of these ingredients.

PIE FILLING DIRECTIONS

1. Add to blender all ingredients except coconut oil and lecithin.
2. Blend well until smooth and creamy (3–5 minutes).
3. Stop blending and add the lecithin and melted coconut oil.
4. Resume blending until oil and lecithin are well incorporated.
5. Pour filling into pie pan with prepared crust.
6. Place in freezer to set, 1–2 hours or until middle of pie is firm to the touch, unless otherwise specified in recipe.
7. Finish and/or garnish pie according to individual recipes, and serve.

USEFUL TIPS

The ingredients subject to the most variability are the nut milks, coconut milk, fresh fruits/vegetables, and the Irish moss. For the Lemon Meringue, Cherry, and Strawberry Brilliance pies, we recommend testing for proper consistency since these pies are primarily set with Irish moss. Do this by pouring a small amount of filling into a ramekin (or small cup) and place in the fridge for 20 minutes. Now, using a small knife, cut into the filling. If the result is a clean cut and the filling is holding its shape, the consistency is perfect. Add tested portion back to blender, blend briefly just enough to reincorporate, and continue with recipe. If tested portion is too loose, add back to blender along with an additional 2 tablespoons coconut oil and blend well. Re-test for consistency. If the tested portion is very gelatinous and hard to the touch, add tested portion back to blender along with 2 tablespoons lemon juice or agave syrup, or a combination of the two. Re-test for consistency.

The most important thing is to blend all ingredients really well. If your blender has less than 8 cups full capacity or if the machine is struggling, blend half the recipe at a time.

If the filling doesn't taste rich and flavorful, add another small pinch of salt and blend a little longer. Always taste the filling before pouring into the crust.

Coconut Cream Pie

Makes one 9-inch pie

COCONUT CRUST

2¼ cups coconut flakes
4½ ounces date paste (weight)
¼ teaspoon liquid vanilla
⅛ teaspoon salt

Process all ingredients. Follow pie crust directions, page 18.

COCONUT FILLING

2¼ cups coconut milk
¾ cup coconut meat (wet measure)
½ cup date paste (wet measure)
2 teaspoons liquid vanilla
⅛ teaspoon salt
2 tablespoons lecithin
½ cup + 2 tablespoons extra-virgin coconut oil

Blend until smooth and creamy. Follow pie filling directions, page 20.

TOPPING

½ cup coconut flakes

Storage and life span: This pie will keep for at least three days. Keep covered in the fridge.

Pecan Pie

Makes one 9-inch pie

MACADAMIA CRUST
3 cups macadamias
⅛ teaspoon salt

Process both ingredients carefully. See basic pie crust directions (page 18) and "Useful Tips" (page 19).

PECAN FILLING
1½ ounces Irish moss (weight)
¾ cup water
¾ cup agave syrup
1½ cups pecans
9 ounces date paste (weight)
2 tablespoons liquid vanilla
2 tablespoons yacon syrup
⅛ teaspoon salt

Blend Irish moss with water and agave until Irish moss is completely broken down. See Irish moss blending directions, page 184. Set aside.

Process pecans first until a paste-like consistency is achieved. Now add to the processed pecans the blended portion of the recipe along with the vanilla, yacon syrup, and salt, and process until smooth. While processing, add the date paste in small amounts. Continue processing until mixture is smooth and dates are completely broken down.

Pour into prepared pie crust and top/decorate with:

1 cup pecans (chopped)

Set in fridge 20–30 minutes.

Storage and life span: This pie will keep for at least three days. Keep covered in the fridge.

Pecan Pie and Coconut Cream Pie (top), Cappuccino Pie and Pumpkin Pie

Pumpkin Pie

Makes one 9-inch pie

PECAN CRUST
3 cups pecans
2½ ounces date paste (weight)
¼ teaspoon vanilla
⅛ teaspoon salt

Process all ingredients. Follow pie crust directions, page 18.

PUMPKIN SPICE FILLING
3 cups raw butternut squash (medium-packed, about 7½
    ounces weight)
1¼ cups coconut milk
6 tablespoons agave syrup
1 tablespoon ginger juice
2 teaspoons cinnamon
2 teaspoons liquid vanilla
½ teaspoon nutmeg
¼ teaspoon clove
⅛ teaspoon turmeric
⅛ teaspoon salt
2 tablespoons lecithin
¾ cups coconut oil

Blend until smooth and creamy. Follow pie filling directions, page
20.

Storage and life span: This pie will keep for at least three days. Keep
covered in the fridge.

Note: Despite the common belief that squash cannot be eaten raw,
it can. Though often hard on digestion, the raw squash in this pie
with all the spices is no problem to digest! Always use fully ripe,
bright yellow-orange squash when making this recipe, or else the
color and flavor will be weak.

Cappuccino Pie

Makes one 9-inch pie

CHOCOLATE-HAZELNUT CRUST
1 cup macadamias
1 cup hazelnuts
4 tablespoons cacao powder
2½ ounces date paste (weight)
4 tablespoons cacao nibs
1 teaspoon liquid vanilla
⅛ teaspoon salt

Process all ingredients. Follow pie crust directions, page 18.

CAPPUCCINO FILLING
1 ounce Irish moss (weight)
¾ cup almond milk

Blend these ingredients until smooth (see Irish moss blending directions, page 184).
    Then add to blender:

¾ cup cold-pressed espresso
¼ cup agave syrup
½ cup pitted dates (wet measurement)
⅓ cup almond milk
3 tablespoons liquid vanilla
2 teaspoons cacao powder
2 tablespoons lecithin
½ cup coconut oil
2 tablespoons cacao butter
⅛ teaspoon salt

Resume blending until mixture is smooth and creamy. Follow pie filling directions, page 20.

MOCHA TOPPING

1 cup Coconut Meringue recipe, page 185
1½ tablespoons cold-pressed espresso
½ tablespoon agave syrup
¼ teaspoon cacao powder
1 teaspoon lecithin
1½ tablespoons cacao butter

First blend the Coconut Meringue by itself to loosen it up. Now add the espresso, agave, and cacao powder and blend until well incorporated. Add the lecithin and cacao butter and resume blending until mixture is consistent. Pour on top of pie and spread evenly. Garnish with cacao powder/nibs or espresso beans and serve!

Storage and life span: This pie will keep for at least four days. Keep covered in the fridge.

Lemon Meringue Pie

Makes one 9-inch pie

MACADAMIA-COCONUT CRUST

1½ cups macadamias
¾ cup cashews
¾ cup coconut flakes
2 ounces date paste (weight)
¼ teaspoon vanilla
⅛ teaspoon salt

Process all ingredients. Follow pie crust directions, page 18.

LEMON FILLING

2 ounces Irish moss (weight)
1 cup + 2 tablespoons lemon juice
6 tablespoons water

Blend all ingredients until smooth (see Irish Moss blending directions, page 184). Then add to blender:

¾ cup agave syrup
⅛ teaspoon turmeric

Resume blending until mixture is smooth and creamy. Add to blender:

2 teaspoons lecithin
6 tablespoons coconut oil

Resume blending until lecithin and oil are well incorporated.

Test for consistency before pouring into pie crust. See "Useful Tips," page 19. Top pie with a thick layer of Coconut Meringue (page 185). Using the back of a spoon, create "peaks" on the meringue.

Storage and life span: This pie will keep for at least three days. Keep covered in the fridge.

Lemon Meringue Pie and Heavenly Mudslide Pie

Heavenly Mudslide Pie

Makes one 9-inch pie

CHOCOLATE-COCONUT CRUST
1½ cups coconut flakes
¾ cup almonds
1½ ounces cacao powder (weight)
4 ounces date paste (weight)
1 tablespoon liquid vanilla
⅛ teaspoon salt

Process all ingredients. Follow pie crust directions, page 18.

WHITE CHOCOLATE FILLING
1¼ cups coconut milk
1 cup soaked cashews (wet measure)
6 tablespoons agave syrup
3 tablespoons liquid vanilla
⅛ teaspoon salt
1½ tablespoons lecithin
6 tablespoons cacao butter

Blend until smooth and creamy. Follow pie filling directions, page 20. Separate 2 cups of this filling for making the Almond Butter Filling. Place remainder of filling in bowl and set in the fridge until ready to fill pie.

ALMOND BUTTER FILLING
2 cups White Chocolate Filling
½ cup almond butter

Blend long enough to evenly incorporate the almond butter. Set in bowl in fridge until ready to fill pie.

CHOCOLATE FILLING
⅓ cup almond milk
3 tablespoons agave syrup
1½ tablespoons cacao powder
2 tablespoons liquid vanilla
⅛ teaspoon salt
1 teaspoon lecithin
2 tablespoons cacao butter

Blend until smooth and creamy. Follow pie filling directions, page 20. Set in bowl in fridge until ready to fill pie.

Once all three fillings are prepared and thickened to the same consistency, they are ready to pour into the pie. The thickness should be that of loose pancake batter. They all need to be set in the fridge until they achieve this consistency. If any of the fillings have set too far, melt down over a hot water bath, stirring constantly until desired consistency is achieved.

Pour the fillings into the prepared crust. Do this in increments, alternating fillings/colors. Swirl the top of the pie once all fillings are poured into the crust. Follow pouring/swirling directions on page 85.

Storage and life span: This pie will keep for at least three days. Keep covered in the fridge.

Key Lime Pie

Makes one 9-inch pie

MACADAMIA-PECAN CRUST
1¼ cups macadamias
1¼ cups pecans
3 ounces date paste (weight)
¼ teaspoon liquid vanilla
⅛ teaspoon salt

Process all ingredients. Follow basic pie crust directions, page 18.

LIME FILLING

¾ cup lime juice

½ cup agave syrup

¼ cup coconut milk

1 cup avocado (wet measure)

2 teaspoons liquid vanilla

⅛ teaspoon salt

2 tablespoons lecithin

½ cup + 2 tablespoons coconut oil

Blend until smooth and creamy. Follow pie filling directions, page 20.

Evenly spread a thin layer of the Coconut Meringue (page 185) on top of the pie. Decorate with lime slices and serve!

Storage and life span: This pie will keep for at least three days. Keep covered in the fridge.

Key Lime Pie and Chocolate-Hazelnut Mousse Pie

Chocolate-Hazelnut Mousse Pie

Makes one 9-inch pie

HAZELNUT-MACADAMIA CRUST
1¼ cups macadamias
1¼ cups hazelnuts
3½ ounces date paste (weight)
¼ teaspoon liquid vanilla
⅛ teaspoon salt

Process all ingredients. Follow pie crust directions, page 18.

CHOCOLATE-HAZELNUT FILLING
¾ ounce Irish moss (weight)
¾ cup hazelnut milk

Blend until Irish moss is completely broken down. See Irish moss blending directions, page 184. Add to blender:

1½ cups hazelnut milk
¼ cup + 2 tablespoons date paste (wet measure)
6 tablespoons agave syrup
1½ ounces cacao powder (weight)
2 tablespoons liquid vanilla
⅛ teaspoon salt
2 tablespoons lecithin
½ cup coconut oil

Blend until smooth and creamy. Follow pie filling directions, page 20.
    Evenly spread a thin layer of the Coconut Meringue (page 185) on top of the pie. Decorate with cacao nibs and hazelnuts.

Storage and life span: This pie will keep for at least three days. Keep covered in the fridge.

Cherry Pie

Makes one 9-inch pie

MACADAMIA CRUST
3 cups macadamias
⅛ teaspoon salt

Process both ingredients carefully. See pie crust directions (page 18) and "Useful Tips" (page 19). Separate ¾ cup of the processed crust and set aside to use for the lattice topping. Use the remaining amount to form the crust. If you are not making a lattice topping use only 2¼ cups macadamias for the crust.

For the lattice topping, use a rolling pin to roll out the ¾ cup of processed macadamias on a non-stick surface. Create somewhat of a rectangular shape about ⅛ inch thick. Carefully cut strips that are a half inch wide, lift them really carefully with a knife, and place them on top of the finished pie, creating a lattice-like effect.

CHERRY FILLING
2¼ ounces Irish moss (weight)
½ cup + 2 tablespoons lemon juice
½ cup + 2 tablespoons agave syrup
4 tablespoons liquid vanilla

Blend all ingredients until smooth (see Irish moss blending directions, page 184). Then add to blender:

1¾ cups pitted cherries (about 11½ ounces weight)
⅛ teaspoon salt

Resume blending until mixture is smooth and creamy. Test for consistency; see "Useful Tips," page 19. Transfer to a bowl and toss with:

2¼ cups pitted, lightly chopped cherries
(about 18 ounces weight)

Stir in the cherries until mixture is consistent. Pour into prepared pie shell and smooth out in an even layer. Set pie in fridge or freezer until firm to the touch. Arrange the lattice topping and serve.

Storage and life span: This pie will keep for at least four days. Keep covered in the fridge.

Strawberry Brilliance Pie

Makes one 9-inch pie

BRAZIL NUT–CASHEW CRUST
1½ cups Brazil nuts
¾ cup cashews
¾ cup coconut flakes
4 ounces date paste (weight)
½ teaspoon liquid vanilla
⅛ teaspoon salt

Process all ingredients. Follow pie crust directions, page 18.

STRAWBERRY FILLING
1¾ ounces Irish moss (weight)
¾ cup agave syrup
6 tablespoons lemon juice
3 tablespoons water

Blend all ingredients until smooth (see Irish moss blending directions, page 184). Then add to blender:

4 cups fresh strawberries (16 ounces weight)
2 teaspoons liquid vanilla
⅛ teaspoon salt

Resume blending until mixture is smooth and creamy. Add to blender:

1 tablespoon lecithin
½ cup coconut oil

Resume blending until mixture is smooth and creamy, and lecithin and oil are well incorporated. Test for consistency; see "Useful Tips," page 19. Set in freezer 30–45 minutes or until center of pie is firm.

STRAWBERRY-MERINGUE TOPPING
1½ cups of the Coconut Meringue recipe (page 185)
2–3 strawberries (about 1½ ounces weight)
½ teaspoon beet juice
1½ tablespoons coconut oil

First blend the Coconut Meringue by itself to loosen it up. Now add the strawberries and beet juice and blend until well incorporated. Add the lecithin and coconut oil and resume blending until mixture is consistent. Pour onto top of pie and spread evenly. Garnish with fresh strawberries and serve!

Strawberry Brilliance Pie

Variations: Substitute the strawberries with other berries like blue-berries or raspberries.

Storage and life span: This pie will keep for at least three days. Keep covered in the fridge.

Apple Pie
Makes one 9-inch pie

MACADAMIA CRUST
3 cups macadamias
⅛ teaspoon salt

Process both ingredients carefully. See pie crust directions (page 18) and "Useful Tips" (page 19).

APPLE FILLING

STEP 1
7 medium-sized apples (30 ounces weight sliced apples)
2½ tablespoons lemon juice
1 teaspoon liquid vanilla
1 teaspoon ginger juice

STEP 2
1¼ cup apple juice

STEP 3
1½ cups apple juice
1 ounce Irish moss (weight)
⅓ cup date paste (3 ounces weight)
1 tablespoon yacon syrup
1 teaspoon cinnamon
⅛ teaspoon nutmeg
1 teaspoon liquid vanilla
⅛ teaspoon salt

WALNUT TOPPING

1 cup walnuts

1½ ounces date paste (weight)

¼ teaspoon liquid vanilla

⅛ teaspoon salt

APPLE FILLING DIRECTIONS

1. Core and slice apples to about ¼-inch thickness. Toss with the lemon, vanilla, and ginger juice. Spread apple slices on dehydrator sheets in a single layer. Dehydrate apples at 145° for 1 hour and then at 115° for another 10 hours.
2. Soak the dehydrated apple slices in the apple juice for about 1 hour or until soft. Strain the apples and reserve the liquid.
3. Blend the Irish moss with 1½ cups of the apple juice (see Irish moss blending directions, page 184). Add the remaining ingredients and resume blending until smooth, thick, and slightly warm. Toss this mixture with the re-hydrated apple slices until well coated. Pour into prepared pie crust and set in fridge until firm.

WALNUT TOPPING DIRECTIONS

Process all ingredients until crumbly and walnuts are still slightly chunky. Sprinkle over the top of the pie.

Storage and life span: This pie will keep for at least four days. Keep covered in the fridge.

Thank you to Arielle Webb for this fantastic recipe!

Apple Pie and Pear, Persimmon, and Pomegranate Cobbler

Fruit Cobbler

Makes one 9x9x2-inch pan of cobbler

WALNUT CRUST/TOPPING

3 cups walnuts
2 ounces date paste (weight)
¼ teaspoon cinnamon
¼ teaspoon liquid vanilla
⅛ teaspoon salt

Process all ingredients until walnuts are still slightly chunky. Once ready, separate the crust into two equal portions. Sprinkle one portion evenly over bottom of pan and lightly compact. Reserve the other portion for the topping.

FRUIT FILLING
**8 cups sliced fruit of your choice
  (any combination of fruit or berries)
2 tablespoons lemon juice
2 tablespoons agave syrup (optional)
1 tablespoon liquid vanilla
1½ teaspoons cinnamon
⅛ teaspoon salt**

FRUIT FILLING DIRECTIONS
Combine all ingredients in a bowl and mix well. Evenly distribute the filling on top of the crust. Then crumble the remaining crust on top of the fruit and gently press. Decorate with fresh fruit slices.

Variations: Use pecans instead of walnuts for the crust/topping. This cobbler lends itself to endless variations of fruit that can be used. Be creative—use what you love and what is in season for the best result. Some of our favorite cobbler combinations are:

Apple/strawberry, white peach/raspberry/mango, pear/persimmon/pomegranate, and berry medley cobbler (blueberry/strawberry/raspberry/blackberry).

Storage and life span: This dessert is best on the day it is made. Over subsequent days the cobbler will begin to juice and the nuts will get soggy. Keep covered in the fridge for up to two days.

Banana Cream Pie

Makes one 9-inch pie

COCONUT CRUST

2¼ cups coconut flakes

4½ ounces date paste (weight)

½ teaspoon liquid vanilla

⅛ teaspoon salt

Process all ingredients. Follow pie crust directions, page 18. Now layer the following on top of the prepared crust:

1 medium-sized banana (cut into thin slices)

BANANA FILLING

1¼ cups coconut milk

1¼ cup bananas (wet measurement, about 3 bananas)

½ cup date paste (wet measurement)

1 tablespoon liquid vanilla

1 teaspoon lemon juice

⅛ teaspoon salt

2 tablespoons lecithin

½ cup + 2 tablespoons coconut oil

Blend until smooth and creamy. Follow pie filling directions, page 20.

NUT-FREE COCONUT TOPPING

½ cup coconut milk

¼ cup coconut meat (wet measure)

2 tablespoons agave syrup

1 teaspoon liquid vanilla

⅛ teaspoon salt

½ tablespoon lecithin

3 tablespoons coconut oil

Thank you to Arielle Webb for this fantastic recipe!

Blend until smooth and creamy. Follow pie filling directions, page 20. Pour on pie and set in freezer for about 30 minutes. Garnish with slices of bananas that have been tossed in a small amount of lemon juice to prevent them from turning dark.

Storage and life span: This pie will keep for at least two days. Keep covered in the fridge.

Note: Use only bananas that are not too ripe or even showing any brown spots on the outside. Bananas that are too ripe will make the filling soft and gray-colored. It will probably still taste fine but not look too appealing.

Neapolitan Tart

Makes one 10-inch tart

CHOCOLATE TART SHELL
1½ cups soaked cashews
½ cup coconut flakes
½ cup macadamias (2½ ounces weight)
2 ounces cacao powder (weight)
3 ounces date paste (weight)
⅛ teaspoon salt
1 tablespoon liquid vanilla

Process all ingredients. Follow cheesecake crust directions, page 82, omitting Step 5. Now, distribute tart shell mixture evenly on the bottom of the pan and create a one-inch wall (about halfway up) on the side. Lightly compact the bottom of the crust. Firmly press around the sides to create the rim of the tart shell. A spoon is helpful to smooth out the top edge.

Chill the tart shell in the freezer for 20 minutes, then remove the springform ring after running a paring knife around the sides. Keep in fridge until ready to be filled.

VANILLA CUSTARD
1½ cups soaked cashews
½ cup coconut meat (4 ounces weight)
¼ cup liquid vanilla
1 vanilla bean (scraped insides only)
½ cup + 2 tablespoons agave syrup
¼ cup almond milk
⅛ teaspoon salt
1 tablespoon lecithin
½ cup coconut oil

Blend until smooth and creamy. Follow pie filling directions, page 20.

FOR THE GLAZED STRAWBERRIES
3½ cups chopped strawberries
1 recipe of the Irish Moss Glaze
   (from the Irish moss chapter), page 189

Layer 1½ cups of the strawberries directly on top of the vanilla custard. Toss the remaining 2 cups of strawberries with the freshly made glaze. Push strawberries slightly into the filling. For best results, toss fruit with glaze immediately, as the glaze will begin to gel right away. Layer glazed berries on top of tart. Set in fridge 20–30 minutes or until glaze has gelled.

Storage and life span: This tart will keep for at least three days. Keep covered in the fridge.

Raspberry Tart

Makes one 9-inch tart

CASHEW-COCONUT TART SHELL
1½ cups soaked cashews
1 cup coconut flakes
½ cup macadamias (2½ ounces weight)
2 ounces date paste (weight)
1 teaspoon liquid vanilla
⅛ teaspoon salt

Process all ingredients. Follow cheesecake crust directions, page 82, omitting Step 5. Now, distribute tart shell mixture evenly on the bottom of the pan and create a one-inch wall (about halfway up) on the side. Lightly compact the bottom of the crust. Firmly press around the sides to create the rim of the tart shell. A spoon is helpful to smooth out the top edge.

Chill the tart shell in the freezer for 20 minutes, then remove the springform ring after running a paring knife around the sides. Keep in fridge until ready to be filled.

LIME CUSTARD
1½ cups soaked cashews
½ cup coconut meat (4 ounces weight)
¼ cup lime juice
½ cup agave syrup
⅛ teaspoon turmeric
¼ cup almond milk
3 tablespoons liquid vanilla
⅛ teaspoon salt
1 tablespoon lecithin
7 tablespoons coconut oil

Blend until smooth and creamy. Follow pie filling directions, page 20.

FOR THE GLAZED RASPBERRIES
3½ cups fresh raspberries
1 recipe of the Irish Moss Glaze, page 189

Layer 1½ cups of the raspberries directly on top of the lime custard. Toss the remaining 2 cups raspberries with the freshly made glaze. Push raspberries slightly into the filling. For best results, toss fruit with glaze immediately, as the glaze will begin to gel right away. Layer glazed berries on top of tart. Set in fridge 20–30 minutes or until glaze has gelled.

Storage and life span: This tart will keep for at least three days. Keep covered in the fridge.

Raspberry Tart with Lime Custard

CHAPTER 3

Cakes

Giving and Receiving

Christmas is the time when many of us are really aware of the acts of giving and receiving, yet the essence of giving and receiving goes far beyond the gesture of exchanging presents. Giving and receiving is an all-encompassing life cycle we share with all beings. Everything on the planet is in some way connected to this cycle and has its own unique place within it, contributing to the overall balance of life. We are constantly giving and receiving something, whether it is material, energetic, action-oriented, or even our thoughts. Giving and receiving is simply the flow of life.

True giving is to give without the expectation of receiving. This kind of giving keeps us connected to the cycle of giving and receiving, offering real fulfillment and meaning to our lives. Equally important is the capability to receive without feeling like we need to give in return. True receiving happens when we are open to accept all that life has to offer and believe that we are worthy of it.

Food is, in general, something that we give and receive all the time. We buy or grow our food, eat it or give it away, and it all goes back to the earth, perpetuating the never-ending cycle of nature. We also receive nourishment from the food we eat, and that nourishment is transformed into energy for us to be able to give.

When food is given as a gift, we often choose a dessert or something sweet. That's because we are naturally more open to the sweet things in life. People more joyfully give and receive desserts and the sweet tokens of affection that they symbolize. Cakes are given as gifts every day of the year. It is the essential gift for many celebrations. Give yourself a break, have a piece of cake!

Our raw cakes are a combination of a whipped "batter," usually layered with a creamy frosting. The base of the batter always consists of dates, nut flour, coconut oil, salt, and vanilla, which are whipped using a mixer (Kitchen Aid). A mixer is indispensable in these recipes to achieve a cake-like result. Fresh fruits, spices, or other flavorings are incorporated into the basic batter for the creation of each unique cake. This approach to raw cake-making often produces a result that is surprisingly better than a conventional baked cake.

The frostings we use generally consist of some type of milk (nut or coconut) or juice blended with soaked cashews and coconut oil. The coconut oil makes the frosting firm and creates an ideal consistency for a layered cake and also for decorating with a pastry bag. Making these cakes involves multiple steps that require more time to accomplish than some of the other desserts in this book; the results, however, are extraordinary and worth the effort.

Recipes

Equipment Needed

- Mixer (Kitchen Aid) with paddle or whip attachment
- Blender (ideally a Vita-Mix blender or something comparable)
- Scale
- Nine-inch cake pan with removable bottom
- Measuring cup (ideally have two 1-quart measuring cups)
- Measuring spoons
- Spatulas
- Piping kit (optional)

Basic Directions

The following general directions aim to help you have a successful experience when making these cakes. We also include useful tips— things you want to pay attention to when making the desserts in this chapter. We often suggest what to look for as a result rather than giving a specific timing for different steps. Please remember that using natural ingredients will create different results. Pay attention to the consistency, color, smell, flavor, and texture of the ingredients you are working with as you go along.

Making the Cake Batter

The basic ingredients you need for the cake batter are:

- Date paste
- Coconut oil (extra virgin or unscented)
- Almond/hazelnut flour
- Liquid vanilla
- Salt

See Chapter 1 for detailed information about these ingredients.

The following directions describe how to whip these ingredients with a mixer and create the desired consistency for the first step of making a cake. Each recipe has additional ingredients that make the cake unique, and each recipe will have specific assembling instructions. Follow these steps and be confident in knowing that we are sharing with you all the tips and techniques that we have found to be most helpful.

CAKE BATTER DIRECTIONS

1. Add to the mixer bowl the date paste, coconut oil, vanilla, and salt.
2. Start mixing at low speed first then higher until you have a creamy and very smooth consistency. This will take a few

minutes. Allow more time if necessary. The result you want is similar to a cookie-dough consistency: light, whipped, and creamy. This process should take 5–15 minutes. If you notice that the mixture is becoming darker in color and has an oily look, then you want to stop mixing and proceed to Step 3.

This is usually the result of over-mixing. No worries, it won't affect the end result.

3. Turn off the mixer and add the nut flour as well as the other ingredients called for (such as milk, juice, cacao powder, etc.). Begin mixing at low speed. Mix for about 5 minutes or until all ingredients are well incorporated. Increase speed to medium or high and continue mixing 5–15 minutes. The cake batter should be soft in consistency and rather light to the touch. Mix longer if the batter feels heavy and not smooth.

4. As the cake is mixing you may want to start the frosting so both components will be ready for the first assembling step.

USEFUL TIPS

The ingredients subject to the most variability are the date paste and flour. *If the cake is too moist:* Unusually moist flour or dates may lead to cake dough that is too wet. If you notice that you are working with moist/wet flour, add the liquid portion of the recipe a little at the time instead of all at once. In this way you'll be able to control how much liquid you need.

Dates that are overly ripe will be really wet. If this happens, simply add a few extra tablespoons of flour to the cake dough and mix longer. If you are making a chocolate cake you may want to add extra cacao powder as well as flour.

If the cake is too dry: When the flour or dates are unusually dry, you may need to add a few extra tablespoons of the liquid that the recipe calls for (milk, juices, espresso, etc.).

Remember to add small quantities at a time. We recommend increments of a few tablespoons until the desired consistency is achieved. You will be surprised how much difference a small quantity of liquid will make.

Always taste the cake batter—the end result should taste delicious! Sample it and ask yourself if there is anything missing (secret ingredient?). Sometimes adding a small pinch of salt is all you need. If you desire a sweeter cake batter, you can add a tablespoon of agave syrup and some extra vanilla. Remember that adding more liquid will affect the consistency.

Making the Frosting

The basic ingredients needed for frostings are:

* Soaked cashews
* Nut/coconut milk or juice
* Agave syrup
* Salt
* Vanilla
* Lecithin
* Coconut oil/Cacao butter

See Chapter 1 for detailed information about these ingredients.

CAKE FROSTING DIRECTIONS

1. Add to blender all ingredients except the coconut oil and lecithin.
2. Blend well until smooth and creamy (3–5 minutes).
3. Stop blending and add the lecithin and melted coconut oil/cacao butter.
4. Resume blending until oil and lecithin are well incorporated. Test frosting for consistency; see "Useful Tips" below.
5. Proceed to cake assembly directions.

The ingredients subject to the most variability are the nut milks and coconut milk.

The most important thing is to blend frostings really well. If your blender has less than 8 cups full capacity or if your blender is struggling, blend half the recipe at a time.

If the frosting doesn't taste rich and flavorful, add another small pinch of salt and blend a little longer.

While you are becoming familiar with these recipes, we recommend testing the frostings for proper consistency before assembling the cake. Do this by pouring a small amount (about one inch thick) into a ramekin or small cup. Place in the freezer 20–30 minutes. After this time, the frosting should be firm to the touch and have thickened throughout. If so, proceed with cake assembly directions (below). If the frosting is still soft, loose and/or runny, you need to add more coconut oil. Add the tested portion back to the blender along with 2 tablespoons coconut oil and blend again until smooth and oil is incorporated. Re-test for consistency.

You don't want the frosting to be frozen. A frozen frosting will always change in texture and appearance, making it harder to work with. Check frosting often as it is setting. As soon as it is firm, transfer it to the fridge.

Cake Assembly Directions

1. Divide cake batter into two equal portions.
2. Lightly grease the cake pan with a little coconut oil.
3. Place one portion of the batter on the bottom of the pan. Spread in an even, flat layer. Keep the remaining cake portion out at room temperature until ready to use.
4. Pour 2½–3 cups of liquid frosting onto first cake layer. This will be the middle layer of frosting in the finished cake.
5. Place cake pan in freezer. Set until frosting is firm (1–2 hours).
6. Pour the remaining frosting in a container, and set in freezer until firm (1–2 hours). Move to fridge once set.

7. Remove cake pan from freezer. Take the remaining portion of cake batter and spread evenly on top of the middle layer of frosting.

8. Set cake in freezer 20–30 minutes.

9. Remove cake from freezer. Insert a non-serrated paring knife along the inside edge of the cake pan. Run the knife around the edge of the cake. Be careful not to cut into the cake.

10. The cake can now be released from the pan. Carefully lift out.

11. Frost the cake to your liking.

Strawberry Shortcake
Makes one 9-inch cake

STRAWBERRY CAKE

24 ounces date paste (weight)

¾ cup coconut oil

3 tablespoons liquid vanilla

1 teaspoon salt

8 cups almond flour

3 cups strawberries (12 ounces weight)

¼ cup lemon juice

1 tablespoon beet juice (for color)

Add to a mixer bowl the date paste, coconut oil, liquid vanilla, and salt and follow the cake batter directions (page 48).

WHIPPED CREAM FROSTING

2 cups soaked cashews

2 cups coconut milk

½ cup agave syrup

1 tablespoon lemon juice

1 tablespoon liquid vanilla

⅛ teaspoon salt

2 tablespoons lecithin

1 cup coconut oil

Follow cake frosting directions, page 50; when frosting is ready, follow cake assembly directions, page 51. When assembling the cake, layer 1½ cups fresh chopped strawberries on top of the first cake layer, pour the frosting on top of the layered strawberries, and continue with cake assembly directions.

Storage and life span: This cake will keep for at least three days. Store covered in the fridge.

Lemon-Poppy Seed Cake

Makes one 9-inch cake

LEMON–POPPYSEED CAKE
24 ounces date paste (weight)
¾ cup coconut oil
3 tablespoons liquid vanilla
1 teaspoon salt
8 cups almond flour
¼ cup almond milk
¾ cup lemon juice
⅓ cup poppy seeds

Add to a mixer bowl the date paste, coconut oil, liquid vanilla, and salt, then follow the cake batter directions, page 48.

LEMON FROSTING
2 cups soaked cashews
1¼ cups almond milk
¾ cup lemon juice
¾ cup agave syrup
1 teaspoon liquid vanilla
⅛ teaspoon salt
3 tablespoons lecithin
1 cup coconut oil

Follow cake frosting directions, page 50; when the frosting is ready follow cake assembly directions, page 51.

Storage and life span: This cake will keep for at least three days. Store covered in the fridge.

Yin & Yang Cake and Lemon–Poppy Seed Cake

Yin & Yang Cake

Makes one 9-inch cake

CHOCOLATE CAKE
24 ounces date paste (weight)
¾ cup coconut oil
4 tablespoons liquid vanilla
1 teaspoon salt
8 cups almond flour
2½ ounces cacao powder (weight)
1 cup almond milk

Add to a mixer bowl the date paste, coconut oil, liquid vanilla, and salt, then follow the cake batter directions (page 48).

WHITE CHOCOLATE FROSTING
2 cups soaked cashews
2 cups coconut milk
½ cup agave syrup
¼ cup liquid vanilla
⅛ teaspoon salt
3 tablespoons lecithin
½ cup coconut oil
½ cup cacao butter

Follow directions for cake frosting on page 50. When the frosting is ready, follow cake assembly directions on page 51.

Storage and life span: This cake will keep for at least three days. Store covered in the fridge.

Mocha Cake

Makes one 9-inch cake

MOCHA CAKE

24 ounces date paste (weight)
¾ cup coconut oil
4 tablespoons liquid vanilla
1 teaspoon salt
8 cups almond flour
2½ ounces cacao powder (weight)
½ cup almond milk
½ cup cold-pressed espresso

Add to a mixer bowl the date paste, coconut oil, liquid vanilla, and salt. Follow the cake batter directions on page 48.

MOCHA CASHEW-FREE FROSTING

1 ounce Irish moss (weight)
1 cup almond milk

Blend until Irish moss is completely broken down. (See Irish moss blending directions, page 184.) Add to blender:

¾ cup almond milk
¾ cup cold-pressed espresso
½ cup agave syrup
½ cup date paste (wet measure)
3 tablespoons cacao powder
3 tablespoons liquid vanilla
⅛ teaspoon salt
3 tablespoons lecithin
1¼ cups coconut oil

Blend well until smooth and creamy. Follow cake frosting directions on page 50. When the frosting is ready, follow cake assembly directions on page 51.

Variation: Try this cake with the following frosting recipe.

CHOCOLATE-HAZELNUT CASHEW-FREE FROSTING

1 ounce Irish moss (weight)
1 cup hazelnut milk

Blend until Irish moss is completely broken down. (See Irish moss blending directions, page 184.) Add to blender:

1½ cups hazelnut milk
½ cup agave syrup
½ cup date paste (wet measurement)
2 ounces cacao powder (weight)
3 tablespoons liquid vanilla
⅛ teaspoon salt
3 tablespoons lecithin
1¼ cups coconut oil

Mocha Wedding Cake with Chocolate-Hazelnut Frosting

Blend well until smooth and creamy. Follow cake frosting directions on page 50. When the frosting is ready, follow cake assembly directions, page 51.

Storage and life span: This cake will keep for at least three days. Store covered in the fridge.

Chocolate-Orange Cake

Makes one 9-inch cake

CHOCOLATE-ORANGE CAKE
24 ounces date paste (weight)
¾ cup coconut oil
¼ cup liquid vanilla
1 teaspoon salt
9 cups hazelnut flour
2½ ounces cacao powder (weight)
1¼ cups orange juice
zest from 2 oranges

Add to a mixer bowl the date paste, coconut oil, liquid vanilla, and salt; follow the cake batter directions, page 48.

CHOCOLATE-ORANGE FROSTING
2 cups soaked cashews
2 cups orange juice
½ cup agave syrup
¼ cup liquid vanilla
2 ounces cacao powder (weight)
zest from 1 orange
⅛ teaspoon salt
3 tablespoons lecithin
¾ cup coconut oil
2 tablespoons cacao butter

Follow cake frosting directions on page 50. When the frosting is ready, follow cake assembly directions on page 51.

Storage and life span: This cake will keep for at least three days. Store covered in the fridge.

See photo on page 44 of Chocolate-Orange Cake at the Harrison Street Café Gratitude (San Francisco)

Coconut-Lemon Cake

Makes one 9-inch cake

COCONUT-LEMON CAKE

24 ounces date paste (weight)
¾ cup extra-virgin coconut oil
3 tablespoons liquid vanilla
1 teaspoon salt
9 cups hazelnut flour
1 cup lemon juice
½ cup dry coconut flakes (measure, then process in coffee grinder)
¾ teaspoon turmeric

Add to a mixer bowl the date paste, extra-virgin coconut oil, liquid vanilla, and salt. Follow cake batter directions on page 48.

COCONUT-LEMON FROSTING

2 cups soaked cashews
1¾ cups coconut milk
½ cup agave syrup
4 tablespoons lemon juice
1 tablespoon liquid vanilla
⅛ teaspoon salt
2 tablespoons lecithin
1 cup extra-virgin coconut oil

Follow cake frosting directions on page 50. When the frosting is ready, follow cake assembly directions on page 51.

Storage and life span: This cake will keep for at least three days. Store covered in the fridge.

Hazelnut Torte

Makes one 9-inch cake

CRUNCHY BOTTOM LAYER
1¼ cups macadamias
¼ cup hazelnuts
2 tablespoons cacao nibs
2 tablespoons cacao powder
3 ounces date paste (weight)
1 teaspoon liquid vanilla
small pinch salt

Process all ingredients until they are mostly broken down but still chunky. Lightly grease cake pan and evenly distribute mixture on bottom of pan. Use gentle pressure to compact the mixture into an even layer.

TORTE
24 ounces date paste (weight)
¾ cup coconut oil
4 tablespoons liquid vanilla
1 teaspoon salt
9 cups hazelnut flour
4 tablespoons cacao powder
¾ cup hazelnut milk

Add to a mixer bowl the date paste, coconut oil, liquid vanilla, and salt, then follow the cake batter directions on page 48.

HAZELNUT FROSTING
2 cups soaked cashews
1¾ cups hazelnut milk
½ cup agave syrup
3 tablespoons liquid vanilla
3 tablespoons cacao powder
⅛ teaspoon salt
3 tablespoons lecithin
½ cup coconut oil
¼ cup cacao butter

Follow cake frosting directions on page 50. When the frosting is ready, follow cake assembly directions on page 51, omitting Step 2.

Storage and life span: This cake will keep for at least three days. Store covered in the fridge.

Carrot-Goji Berry Cake

Makes one 9-inch cake

CARROT–GOJI BERRY CAKE
22 ounces (weight) date paste (about 3 cups)
¾ cup coconut oil
3 tablespoons liquid vanilla
1 teaspoon salt
8 cups almond flour
1 cup almond milk (or carrot juice)
1 tablespoon cinnamon
1 teaspoon nutmeg
½ teaspoon clove
2 cups carrots (grated)
1 cup walnuts
½ cup goji berries (for softer berries, soak them in warm
      water for about 10 minutes)

Add to a mixer bowl the date paste, coconut oil, liquid vanilla, and salt. Follow the cake batter directions on page 48.

CREAM CHEESE FROSTING
2½ cups soaked cashews
1½ cups almond milk
¾ cup agave syrup
¼ cup lemon juice
1 tablespoon liquid vanilla
⅛ teaspoon salt
3 tablespoons lecithin
1 cup coconut oil

Follow cake frosting directions on page 50 When the frosting is ready, follow cake assembly directions on page 51.

Storage and life span: This cake will keep for at least three days. Store covered in the fridge.

Coffee Cake

Makes one 9-inch cake

ORANGE-CINNAMON CAKE
20 ounces date paste (weight)
⅔ cup coconut oil
2 tablespoons liquid vanilla
½ teaspoon salt
7 cups almond flour
¾ cup orange juice
1 tablespoon cinnamon

Add to a mixer bowl the date paste, coconut oil, liquid vanilla, and salt. Follow the cake batter directions on page 48.

PECAN-GRANOLA TOPPING

5 cups Raw Buckwheat Granola (see recipe on page 129)
2 cups pecans
6 ounces date paste (weight)
⅓ cup agave syrup

COFFEE CAKE TOPPING DIRECTIONS

Add to food processor and lightly process (keep a crunchy consistency) the granola and pecans. Set aside in a bowl.

Add to food processor the date paste and agave and process until smooth and creamy.

Add processed dates and agave to granola-pecan mixture and mix well with a spatula.

ASSEMBLING THE COFFEE CAKE

Place all the cake batter in a cake pan. Gently cover with the topping without using too much pressure, as this may create a dense, hard-to-cut topping. Decorate with Coffee Cake Caramel (recipe below).

COFFEE CAKE CARAMEL

1 recipe of Macadamia Caramel without yacon syrup
   (see page 127)
1 tablespoon coconut oil
½ tablespoon lecithin

Blend well until smooth and creamy (about 5 minutes). Pour caramel into a bowl or squeeze bottle and chill in freezer for 15 minutes. Drizzle Coffee Cake Caramel on top of the chilled cake and serve.

Storage and life span: This cake will keep for at least three days. Store covered in the fridge.

Carrot–Goji Berry Cake (top),
and Coffee Cake

Chocolate-Port Cake

Makes one 9-inch cake

CHOCOLATE-PORT CAKE

24 ounces date paste (weight)
¾ cup coconut oil
4 tablespoons liquid vanilla
1 teaspoon salt
9 cups hazelnut flour
2½ ounces cacao powder (weight)
¾ cup hazelnut milk
½ cup port

Add to a mixer bowl the date paste, coconut oil, liquid vanilla, and salt. Follow the cake batter directions on page 48.

CHOCOLATE-PORT FROSTING

2 cups soaked cashews
2 cups hazelnut milk
½ cup agave syrup
¼ cup liquid vanilla
3½ ounces cacao powder (weight)
1 tablespoon port
⅛ teaspoon salt
3 tablespoons lecithin
¾ cup coconut oil
2 tablespoons cacao butter

Thank you to Daniel Korson for this fantastic recipe!

Follow cake frosting directions on page 50. When the frosting is ready, follow cake assembly directions on page 51. When assembling the cake, soak each cake layer with ¼ cup of port before pouring the chocolate frosting.

Storage and life span: This cake will keep for at least three days. Store covered in the fridge.

German Chocolate Cake

Makes one 9-inch cake

CHOCOLATE-COCONUT CAKE

20 ounces date paste (weight)

¾ cup extra-virgin coconut oil

4 tablespoons liquid vanilla

½ teaspoon salt

9 cups almond flour

2½ ounces cacao powder (weight)

½ cup coconut milk

Add to a mixer bowl the date paste, extra-virgin coconut oil, liquid vanilla, and salt, then follow the cake batter directions on page 48.

WALNUT-COCONUT FILLING

5 cups walnuts

1 cup agave syrup

2 tablespoons liquid vanilla

¼ teaspoon salt

3 cups coconut flakes

Process until smooth 4 cups walnuts (leave 1 cup out for next step), agave, liquid vanilla, and salt. In a bowl combine with a spatula the processed mixture and the remaining 1 cup walnuts with 3 cups coconut flakes.

This filling is a substitute for frosting. Follow cake assembly directions (page 51), using this filling instead of frosting. Use half of this filling in between cake layers and the other half for the top. Since this is a solid filling there is no setting time required, and you can assemble the whole cake at once simply by alternating cake and filling.

When the cake and filling are assembled, set cake in the freezer 15–20 minutes. This will prepare the cake for the final layer of Chocolate Glaze.

CHOCOLATE GLAZE
¾ cup almond milk
½ cup cacao nibs
1½ ounces cacao powder (weight)
½ cup agave syrup
3 ounces date paste (weight)
4 tablespoons liquid vanilla
¼ teaspoon salt
1 tablespoon lecithin
2 tablespoons extra-virgin coconut oil

Follow cake frosting directions on page 50. Let the Chocolate Glaze set in the fridge 15–20 minutes before using.

Pour all the glaze on top of the chilled cake and set in fridge 10–15 minutes. Decorate the cake with coconut flakes and cacao beans/nibs.

Storage and life span: This cake will keep for at least three days. Store covered in the fridge.

German Chocolate Cake

Banana-Walnut Cake

Makes one 9-inch cake

BANANA-WALNUT CAKE

24 ounces date paste (weight)

¾ cup coconut oil

3 tablespoons liquid vanilla

1 teaspoon salt

8 cups hazelnut flour

3 bananas (about 19 ounces weight before peeling)

2½ ounces cacao powder (weight)

1 cup walnuts

Add to a mixer bowl the date paste, coconut oil, liquid vanilla, and salt. Follow the cake batter directions on page 48.

CREAM CHEESE FROSTING

2½ cups soaked cashews

1½ cups almond milk

¾ cup agave syrup

¼ cup lemon juice

1 tablespoon liquid vanilla

3 tablespoons lecithin

1 cup coconut oil

Follow cake frosting directions on page 50. When the frosting is ready, follow cake assembly directions on page 51.

Storage and life span: This cake will keep for at least three days. Store covered in the fridge.

Pumpkin Cake
Makes one 9-inch cake

PUMPKIN CAKE
24 ounces date paste (weight)
¾ cup coconut oil
4 tablespoons liquid vanilla
1 teaspoon salt
8 cups almond flour
Butternut squash mixture (see recipe below)

Add to a mixer bowl the date paste, coconut oil, liquid vanilla, and salt. Follow the cake batter directions on page 48.

BUTTERNUT SQUASH MIXTURE AND DIRECTIONS
3 cups shredded butternut squash (7½ ounces weight)
1 cup coconut milk
¼ cup agave syrup
¼ cup fresh ginger juice
1 tablespoon + 1 teaspoon cinnamon
1½ teaspoons nutmeg
½ teaspoon clove
¼ teaspoon turmeric

Place all ingredients in a blender and blend well until smooth and creamy. When ready, add to the cake batter and keep following the basic cake batter directions.

CREAM CHEESE FROSTING
2½ cups soaked cashews
1½ cups almond milk
¾ cup agave syrup
¼ cup lemon juice
1 tablespoon liquid vanilla
3 tablespoons lecithin
1 cup coconut oil

Follow cake frosting directions on page 50. When the frosting is ready, follow cake assembly directions on page 51.

Storage and life span: This cake will keep for at least three days. Store covered in the fridge.

Chai Spice–Orange Cake

Makes one 9-inch cake

CHAI SPICE CAKE

24 ounces date paste (weight)
¾ cup coconut oil
3 tablespoons liquid vanilla
1 teaspoon salt
9 cups almond flour
½ cup almond milk
½ cup strong chai tea (use 2 teabags)
1 tablespoon cinnamon
1 teaspoon nutmeg

Add to a mixer bowl the date paste, coconut oil, liquid vanilla, and salt and follow the cake batter directions, page 48.

ORANGE FROSTING

2½ cups soaked cashews
2 cups orange juice
¼ cup lemon juice
⅔ cup agave syrup
¼ teaspoon salt
1 tablespoon liquid vanilla
⅛ teaspoon turmeric
3 tablespoons lecithin
1 cup coconut oil

Follow cake frosting directions, page 50; when the frosting is ready follow cake assembly directions, page 51.

Storage and life span: This cake will keep for at least three days. Store covered in the fridge.

Chai Spice–Orange Cake

Aloha Cake

Makes one 9-inch cake

CRUNCHY BOTTOM LAYER
¾ cup macadamias
¾ cup coconut flakes
1 ounce date paste (weight)
1 tablespoon liquid vanilla
⅛ teaspoon salt

Process all ingredients until they are mostly broken down but still chunky. Lightly grease cake pan and evenly distribute mixture on bottom of pan. Use gentle pressure to compact the mixture into an even layer.

TROPICAL CAKE
20 ounces date paste (weight)
¾ cup extra-virgin coconut oil
3 tablespoons liquid vanilla
½ teaspoon salt
8 cups almond flour
¼ cup orange juice
½ teaspoon orange zest
2 tablespoons lime juice
1 cup sliced pineapple

Add to a mixer bowl the date paste, extra-virgin coconut oil, liquid vanilla, and salt. Follow the cake batter directions, page 48.

PINEAPPLE-CARAMEL-COCONUT FILLING
4 cups sliced pineapple
2 cups coconut flakes
⅛ teaspoon salt
1 recipe Macadamia Caramel without yacon syrup
   (see page 127)
½ cup extra-virgin coconut oil

Make Macadamia Caramel, add the extra-virgin coconut oil, and blend until oil is well incorporated. Transfer to a bowl and toss with the pineapple, coconut flakes, and salt.

This filling is a substitute for frosting. Follow cake assembly directions on page 51, omitting step 2, using this filling instead of frosting.

Storage and life span: This cake will keep for at least three days. Store covered in the fridge.

Chocolate-Raspberry Cake

Makes one 9-inch cake

CHOCOLATE CAKE
24 ounces date paste (weight)
¾ cup coconut oil
4 tablespoons liquid vanilla
1 teaspoon salt
8 cups almond flour
3 ounces cacao powder (weight)
1 cup almond milk

Add to a mixer bowl the date paste, coconut oil, liquid vanilla, and salt and follow the cake batter directions, page 48.

RASPBERRY FROSTING
2½ cups soaked cashews
3½ cups fresh raspberries (14 ounces)
¾ cup agave syrup
½ cup almond milk
¼ cup lemon juice
1 tablespoon liquid vanilla

1 tablespoon beet juice

⅛ teaspoon salt

3 tablespoons lecithin

1 cup coconut oil

Follow cake frosting directions, page 50. When the frosting is ready, follow cake assembly directions on page 51.

Storage and life span: This cake will keep for at least three days. Store covered in the fridge.

Chocolate-Raspberry Cake

Tiramisu

Makes one 8x8x2-inch square pan

VANILLA-ESPRESSO CAKE
13 ounces date paste (weight)
7 tablespoons coconut oil
1½ tablespoons liquid vanilla
½ teaspoon salt
4½ cups almond flour
¼ cup almond milk
¼ cup cold-pressed espresso

Add to a mixer bowl the date paste, coconut oil, liquid vanilla, and salt, then follow the cake batter directions on page 48. Save espresso for the soaking of the cake layers.

When cake batter is ready, divide it into two equal parts. Lightly grease the pan and spread one portion of the batter on the bottom in an even, flat layer. Keep the remaining cake portion out at room temperature until ready to use. Soak the cake layer in the pan with 2 tablespoons of the espresso. Place pan in fridge while making the mousse recipe below.

TIRAMISU CHOCOLATE MOUSSE
½ ounce Irish moss (weight)
¼ cup water
½ cup almond milk

Blend until Irish moss is completely broken down (see Irish moss blending directions, page 184). Then add the following to the blender:

½ cup almond milk
¼ cup agave syrup
1½ ounces date paste (weight)
¾ ounce cacao powder (weight)
1½ tablespoons liquid vanilla
small pinch salt

Tiramisu

Blend well until smooth and creamy, then add:

1 tablespoon lecithin
3 tablespoons coconut oil

Resume blending until lecithin and oil are fully incorporated. Pour the mousse on top of the first cake layer. Place entire pan in freezer to set the mousse (45 minutes–1 hour). While mousse is setting, proceed with making the whipped cream recipe below.

When the mousse feels firm, remove pan from freezer and gently apply the second cake layer. Soak second cake layer with remaining 2 tablespoons espresso.

TIRAMISU WHIPPED CREAM
1 cup soaked cashews
1½ cups coconut milk
¼ cup agave syrup
1 teaspoon liquid vanilla
small pinch salt
1½ tablespoons lecithin
⅓ cup coconut oil

Follow cake frosting directions, page 50. When the whipped cream is ready, pour on top of the second cake layer and set in the freezer 1–2 hours or until the whipped cream feels firm to the touch. Decorate the entire top layer with:

6 tablespoons cacao powder

Using a small sifter, gently sift the cacao powder in an even layer on top of the cake. The cacao powder should completely cover the frosting.

Tiramisu is now ready to be served. Score pan 3x3 to yield nine servings. Garnish individual slices with a whole cacao bean or almond for an extra touch. Use an offset spatula to remove servings from the pan.

Storage and life span: This cake will keep for at least three days. Store covered in the fridge.

CHAPTER 4

Cheesecakes

Guilt-Free

Let's release all guilt about our food choices, especially desserts. Whatever we choose, let's choose it powerfully and free from guilt. Choosing something and then feeling guilty about it is not choosing powerfully. Choosing something without judging yourself is freedom from guilt. We empower our experience by celebrating our choices and by choosing freedom from guilt over judgment. Making ourselves wrong for any decision we make prevents us from being in touch with what that experience has to offer.

Few food choices are connected to guilt as much as desserts. We hope to inspire people to fully enjoy every aspect of their diet, especially desserts. Desserts are soul food, celebratory foods that nourish our emotions and lift our spirits, and ours are actually whole foods that are good for you!

We want to acknowledge that desserts are an important part of life, richly steeped in the traditions and rituals of most every culture. Desserts have a symbolic presence during the holidays and milestone celebrations throughout our lives. They remind us of the sweetness and joy of life. Let's enjoy it!

In raw cuisine, cashew nuts are often used as the base for an assortment of raw "cheeses," including cheesecakes. Cashews have a wonderful balance of sweet and savory flavors, as well as being creamy and white in color, making a perfect imitation of a creamy white cheese. Adding lemon for its sour/tart flavor results in a cheese-like taste. Cashew nut cheeses can also be successfully cultured, with extraordinary results. All of our cheesecake recipes use soaked cashews as the base for the filling. Coconut oil gives the cheesecake a firm consistency. The crust we use the most is almond- and date-based. Almonds processed simply with dates, salt, and vanilla produce a yummy, graham cracker-like crust. The filling is blended and then poured onto the crust, set in the freezer, and voila! You have cheesecake. We have created endless different flavors of raw cheesecakes (use your own creativity to find more), but offered here are the real winners—the cream (cheese) of the crop. You are cherished!

Recipes

Equipment Needed

- ◆ Blender
- ◆ Food processor
- ◆ Measuring cups
- ◆ Measuring spoons
- ◆ Scale
- ◆ Spatulas
- ◆ 9- or 10-inch springform pan

Making the Cheesecake Crust

The basic ingredients you need for the cheesecake crust are:

- Nuts (usually almonds)
- Salt
- Date paste
- Liquid vanilla
- Any additional ingredient the recipe calls for (such as cacao powder)

See Chapter 1 for detailed information about these ingredients.

CHEESECAKE CRUST DIRECTIONS

1. Add to food processor the nuts, salt, vanilla, half the amount of date paste, and any other ingredients the recipe may call for.
2. Process all ingredients until the crust starts to rise on the sides of the processor bowl. Stop the machine and mix with a spatula or spoon.
3. Repeat a few times until nuts are well broken down. Add remaining date paste and continue processing until mixture is consistent. The final result of the crust should be a mixture that can hold together with a gentle pressure and can be broken apart with a clean break.
4. Assemble the cheesecake pan with the bottom up (opposite the way it would normally be used with lip facing down). This makes it much easier to serve. Lightly grease the entire inside of the pan with coconut oil.
5. Distribute crust evenly on the bottom of pan and lightly compact by hand. Set aside until ready to be filled.

USEFUL TIPS

If the nuts are too chunky, first try sharpening the "S" blade of your processor. You can also lightly process the nuts and salt by themselves before adding other ingredients. Adding all the date paste at once will not allow the nuts to break down properly.

When pressing crust into pan, be careful not to use too much pressure, as this will result in the crust sticking to the pan and making the serving process challenging. On the other hand, if you are not pressing firmly enough the crust will be crumbly and messy. If crust is not sticking together and breaking apart cleanly, you need to add a small splash (½–1 teaspoon) of liquid vanilla and process a bit longer.

Making the Cheesecake Fillings

The basic ingredients needed for cheesecake fillings are:

* Soaked cashews
* Nut milk, coconut milk, juices, or fresh fruits
* Agave syrup
* Salt
* Liquid vanilla
* Lecithin
* Coconut oil
* Any additional ingredient the recipe calls for (such as cacao powder, espresso, etc.)

See Chapter 1 for detailed information about these ingredients.

CHEESECAKE FILLING DIRECTIONS

1. Add to blender all ingredients except the coconut oil and lecithin.
2. Blend well until smooth and creamy (3–5 minutes).
3. Stop blending and add the lecithin and melted coconut oil.
4. Resume blending until oil and lecithin are well incorporated.
5. Pour filling into springform pan with prepared crust. Recipe may call for a swirling decoration; see swirling instructions below.
6. Place in freezer to set 1–2 hours or until middle of cheesecake is firm to the touch.

7. Remove springform ring by inserting a non-serrated paring knife along the inside edge of pan. Open springform, remove cheesecake, and decorate to your liking.

USEFUL TIPS

The ingredients subject to the most variability are the nut milks and coconut milk.

The most important thing is to blend all ingredients really well. If your blender has less than 8 cups' full capacity or if your blender is struggling, blend half the recipe at a time.

If the filling doesn't taste rich and flavorful, add another small pinch of salt and blend a little longer. Due to human error, measurements can sometimes be inaccurate. When making cheesecake fillings, be aware of what the total cup volume is in the blender before adding the coconut oil. If the total volume is 6 cups or more, always add 1 cup coconut oil for those recipes that call for ¾ cup.

Cashew measurement is intended to be medium-packed, meaning you should lightly press down on cashews when measuring

How to Create a Beautiful Swirl

Swirling is a decorating technique we love and utilize often. Cheesecakes are especially suited for this technique. It is a quick, easy way to make a dessert look surprisingly elegant and delicious. It takes just a little bit of practice to perfect, but the following tips and guidelines will dispel some of the mystery around this technique and make swirling an easy process.

Swirling always requires two or more contrasting colors. The stronger the contrast between the colors, the more striking and beautiful the swirl will be. The swirling components will always be liquid, creamy fillings. There can be multiple fillings, which are entirely different in composition and color (like the Heavenly Mudslide Pie, page 28), or it can be one filling with a portion altered in color by an added ingredient (such as adding cacao powder to a portion of a cheesecake filling).

The basic rule to creating a beautiful swirl is to have each of the fillings as close to the same consistency as possible. This causes them to smoothly and easily flow and glide into each other. The process is very simple. The following measurements are intended for our 10-inch cheesecake recipes.

Swirled fillings of Heavenly Mudslide Pie

POURING/SWIRLING DIRECTIONS

1. Pour all but 2 cups (or amount specified in recipe) of the finished filling into the pan (onto prepared crust).

2. Blend the reserved 2 cups with whatever ingredient the recipe calls for (or that you decide to use). This should be a brief blending phase, as you just need to combine the added ingredient. Often the recipe will call for some additional liquid (like liquid vanilla) to compensate for the added dry ingredient.

3. Now, confidently begin to pour into the pan (only pour about 1½ cups total at this point). Do not pour lightly. You want some of the colored mixture to pierce through the surface of the filling, moving around to evenly distribute throughout the cheesecake. This will create a marbled effect on the inside of the cheesecake, which will be visible on the individual slices.

4. After about 1½ cups have been poured, start to pour very lightly, letting a ribbon of filling fall to the surface. Once you start pouring lightly, the colored filling should sit right on top. Continue to evenly pour the rest of the filling, making sure to touch parts of the edges but not the entire edge.

5. Now you are ready to swirl. A chopstick (or something comparable) is the best tool to use for this purpose. Insert the chopstick just below the surface and begin moving it around, swirling the fillings into each other. Try to make it as balanced as possible, meaning both colors are equally visible. It is important to know when to stop, as too much swirling will blend everything together and you will lose the contrast of the colors. Actual swirling time is very minimal; the effect is achieved quickly. Remember to be confident and that practice makes perfect.

USEFUL TIPS

If you want only the very top of the dessert to have some light swirling, you will only need about ½–¾ cup of colored filling to swirl with. Some recipes will call for this amount. Follow the above directions, omitting Step 3.

Reserve one or more tablespoons of both fillings to do touch-up work on your swirling design if necessary.

Ingredients you can add to fillings to change the color in order to swirl are: cacao powder, spices, vanilla bean, berries, beet juice, or other brightly colored juice.

Lemon Cheesecake

Makes one 10-inch cheesecake

ALMOND CRUST

2 cups almonds
3 ounces date paste (weight)
¼ teaspoon liquid vanilla
⅛ teaspoon salt

Process all ingredients. See cheesecake crust directions on page 82.

LEMON FILLING

3 cups soaked cashews
1½ cups almond milk
1 cup lemon juice
¾ cup agave syrup
1 tablespoon liquid vanilla
3 tablespoons lecithin
¾ cup coconut oil

Blend ingredients until smooth and creamy. Follow cheesecake filling directions on page 83.

Variations: Add almost any kind of fresh fruit to this cheesecake, either inside or layered on the surface. Any kind of berry is fantastic with the lemon cheesecake, especially blueberries.

Storage and life span: Cheesecakes will keep for at least four days. Store covered in the fridge.

Lemon and Mocha Cheesecakes

Mocha Cheesecake

Makes one 10-inch cheesecake

CHOCOLATE-ALMOND CRUST

1¾ cups dry almonds
5 tablespoons cacao powder
3½ ounces date paste (weight)
1 teaspoon liquid vanilla
⅛ teaspoon salt

Process all ingredients. See cheesecake crust directions, page 82.

MOCHA FILLING
3 cups soaked cashews
1¼ cups espresso
¾ cup almond milk
1 cup agave syrup
2 ounces cacao powder (weight)
¼ cup liquid vanilla
¼ teaspoon salt
3 tablespoons lecithin
1¼ cups coconut butter

Blend ingredients until smooth and creamy. Follow cheesecake filling directions on page 83. Try serving/decorating with the Raw Chocolate Sauce recipe, page 161.

Storage and life span: Cheesecakes will keep for at least four days. Store covered in the fridge.

Note: Allow almost double the time for this cheesecake to fully set. Espresso in these recipes increases the setting time substantially.

Orange-Persimmon Cheesecake

Makes one 10-inch cheesecake

HAZELNUT-ALMOND CRUST
1 cup hazelnuts
1 cup almonds
3 ounces date paste (weight)
1 teaspoon liquid vanilla
⅛ teaspoon salt

Process all ingredients. See cheesecake crust directions, page 82. Now layer the following on top of the prepared crust:

1½ cups sliced persimmon (ideally use firm persimmon)

ORANGE-PERSIMMON FILLING

2½ cups soaked cashews

1½ cups sliced persimmon (about 15 ounces weight; use riper/soft persimmon)

1½ cups orange juice

¾ cup agave syrup

1 tablespoon liquid vanilla

⅛ teaspoon salt

3 tablespoons lecithin

1¼ cups coconut oil

1 tablespoon yacon syrup (reserve for final swirling decoration)

Follow cheesecake filling directions on page 83. After pouring the filling, lightly drizzle the yacon syrup over the top and lightly swirl with a chopstick.

Storage and life span: Cheesecakes will keep for at least four days. Store covered in the fridge.

Orange-Persimmon and Pear-Ginger Cheesecakes

Pear-Ginger Cheesecake

Makes one 10-inch cheesecake

CHOCOLATE-ALMOND CRUST

1¾ cups dry almonds

5 tablespoons cacao powder

3½ ounces date paste (weight)

1 teaspoon liquid vanilla

⅛ teaspoon salt

Process all ingredients. See cheesecake crust directions, page 82.

PEAR-GINGER FILLING

3 cups soaked cashews

3 cups chopped pears (about 16 ounces weight)

¾ cup agave syrup

¾ cup ginger juice

½ cup almond milk

2 tablespoons lemon juice

1 tablespoon liquid vanilla

¼ teaspoon cinnamon

¼ teaspoon salt

3 tablespoons lecithin

1 cup coconut oil

Thank you to Zoi Hall for this fantastic recipe!

Blend ingredients until smooth and creamy. Follow directions for cheesecake filling on page 83.

Swirling Variation: For an elegant gourmet touch to this recipe, reserve 1 cup of filling for swirling and add the following:

1½ teaspoons cinnamon

3–4 vanilla beans (scraped insides only)

Follow pouring/swirling directions on page 85.

Storage and life span: Cheesecakes will keep for at least four days. Store covered in the fridge.

Strawberry Cheesecake

Makes one 10-inch cheesecake

ALMOND CRUST

2 cups almonds

3 ounces date paste (weight)

¼ teaspoon liquid vanilla

⅛ teaspoon salt

Process all ingredients. See cheesecake crust directions on page 82.

STRAWBERRY FILLING

3 cups soaked cashews

4 cups strawberries (18 ounces weight)

¾ cup almond milk

¾ cup agave syrup

⅓ cup lemon juice

1 tablespoon liquid vanilla

¼ teaspoon salt

3 tablespoons lecithin

1 cup coconut oil

Blend ingredients until smooth and creamy. Follow cheesecake filling directions on page 83. Garnish with fresh strawberry slices and serve!

Storage and life span: Cheesecakes will keep for at least four days. Store covered in the fridge.

Coconut-Lime and Strawberry Cheesecakes

Coconut-Lime Cheesecake

Makes one 10-inch cheesecake

COCONUT-ALMOND CRUST

1½ cups dry almonds

½ cup coconut flakes

3 ounces date paste (weight)

¼ teaspoon liquid vanilla

⅛ teaspoon salt

Process all ingredients. See cheesecake crust directions, page 82.

COCONUT-LIME FILLING

3 cups soaked cashews

1½ cups coconut milk

1 cup lime juice

¾ cup agave syrup

2 teaspoons liquid vanilla

¼ teaspoon salt

3 tablespoons lecithin

¾ cup extra-virgin coconut oil

Blend ingredients until smooth and creamy. Follow cheesecake filling directions on page 83.

Storage and life span: Cheesecakes will keep for at least four days. Store covered in the fridge.

White Chocolate Cheesecake

Makes one 10-inch cheesecake

CHOCOLATE-ALMOND CRUST

1¾ cups dry almonds

5 tablespoons cacao powder

3½ ounces date paste (weight)

1 teaspoon liquid vanilla

⅛ teaspoon salt

Process all ingredients. See cheesecake crust directions on page 82.

WHITE CHOCOLATE FILLING

3 cups soaked cashews

2 cups almond milk

3 tablespoons lemon juice

¾ cup agave syrup

4 tablespoons liquid vanilla

¼ teaspoon salt

3 tablespoons lecithin
½ cup cacao butter
¼ cup coconut oil

Blend ingredients until smooth and creamy. Follow directions for cheesecake filling on page 83.

Storage and life span: Cheesecakes will keep for at least four days. Store covered in the fridge.

White Chocolate–Raspberry Cheesecake

Makes one 10-inch cheesecake

CHOCOLATE-ALMOND CRUST
¾ cup almonds
¾ cup coconut flakes
1½ ounces cacao powder (weight)
5 ounces date paste (weight)
⅓ cup cacao nibs
2 teaspoons liquid vanilla
⅛ teaspoon salt

Process all ingredients. See cheesecake crust directions on page 82. Now layer the following on top of the prepared crust:

1 pack raspberries (about 6 ounces weight)

WHITE CHOCOLATE FILLING
3 cups soaked cashews
2 cups almond milk
¾ cup agave syrup
2 tablespoons lemon juice
¼ cup liquid vanilla
¼ teaspoon salt
3 tablespoons lecithin
⅔ cup cacao butter

Follow cheesecake filling directions on page 83. Reserve 2 cups of filling for swirling and add the following:

1 pack raspberries (about 6 ounces weight)
2 tablespoons lemon juice

Follow pouring/swirling directions on page 85.

Variations: Substitute other berries for the raspberries, such as blueberries or blackberries.

Storage and life span: Cheesecakes will keep for at least four days. Store covered in the fridge.

White Chocolate–Raspberry Cheesecake

Banana-Chocolate Cheesecake

Makes one 10-inch cheesecake

CHOCOLATE-PECAN CRUST

1½ cups pecans
2 ounces cacao powder (weight)
⅓ cup cacao nibs
4 ounces date paste (weight)
⅛ teaspoon salt
1 tablespoon liquid vanilla

Process all ingredients. See cheesecake crust directions, page 82.

CHOCOLATE-BANANA FILLING

2 cups soaked cashews
2 cups banana (packed, 15 ounces weight)
2 tablespoons lemon juice
¾ cup agave syrup
2 tablespoons liquid vanilla
⅛ teaspoon salt
1 cup almond milk
3 tablespoons lecithin
1 cup coconut oil

Follow cheesecake filling directions on page 83. Reserve 2 cups of filling for swirling and add the following:

1 ounce cacao powder (weight)
1 tablespoon liquid vanilla

Follow pouring/swirling directions on page 85.

Storage and life span: Cheesecakes will keep for at least four days. Store covered in the fridge.

Chai Spice–Chocolate Cheesecake

Makes one 10-inch cheesecake

CHOCOLATE-ALMOND CRUST

1¾ cups dry almonds
5 tablespoons cacao powder
3½ ounces date paste (weight)
1 teaspoon liquid vanilla
⅛ teaspoon salt

Process all ingredients. See cheesecake crust directions on page 82.

CHOCOLATE CHAI FILLING

3 cups soaked cashews
1¼ cups chai
¾ cup almond milk
¾ cup agave syrup
2 tablespoons liquid vanilla
1 tablespoon + 1 teaspoon cinnamon
1¼ teaspoons nutmeg
½ teaspoon cardamom
¼ teaspoon salt
3 tablespoons lecithin
1 cup coconut oil

Thank you to Estevan Sifuentes for this fantastic recipe!

Follow directions for cheesecake filling on page 83. Reserve ¾ cup of filling for swirling and add the following:

2 tablespoons cacao powder

Follow pouring/swirling directions on page 85.

Storage and life span: Cheesecakes will keep for at least four days. Store covered in the fridge.

Chocolate-Orange Cheesecake

Makes one 10-inch cheesecake

CHOCOLATE-ALMOND CRUST

1¾ cups dry almonds

5 tablespoons cacao powder

3½ ounces date paste (weight)

1 teaspoon liquid vanilla

⅛ teaspoon salt

Process all ingredients. See cheesecake crust directions on page 82.

CHOCOLATE-ORANGE FILLING

3 cups soaked cashews

2¼ cups orange juice

¾ cup agave syrup

2 ounces cacao powder (weight)

¼ cup liquid vanilla

zest from 1 orange

¼ teaspoon salt

3 tablespoons lecithin

⅔ cup coconut oil

⅓ cup cacao butter

Blend ingredients until smooth and creamy. Follow cheesecake filling directions on page 83.

Storage and life span: Cheesecakes will keep for at least four days. Store covered in the fridge.

Mint-Chip Cheesecake

Makes one 10-inch cheesecake

CHOCOLATE-ALMOND CRUST

¾ cup dry almonds

¾ cup coconut flakes

1½ ounces cacao powder (weight)

¼ cup cacao nibs

4 ounces date paste (weight)

2 teaspoons liquid vanilla

⅛ teaspoon salt

Process all ingredients. See cheesecake crust directions on page 82.

CHOCOLATE-MINT FILLING

3 cups soaked cashews

2¼ cups almond milk

1 cup agave syrup

¼ cup lemon juice

3 bunches of mint, leaves only

2 tablespoons liquid vanilla

2 teaspoons green food (we use Vitamineral Green by
    HealthForce Nutritionals)

¼ teaspoon salt

3 tablespoons lecithin

1 cup coconut oil

Follow cheesecake filling directions on page 83. Reserve 2 cups of filling for swirling and add:

4 tablespoons cacao powder

1 tablespoon liquid vanilla

Follow pouring/swirling directions on page 85. Finish with:

½ cup cacao nibs

Mint-Chip (top)
and Pecan Turtle Cheesecakes

Apply nibs to the sides of the cheesecake. Do this by carefully holding the cheesecake from the bottom over a counter; take small handfuls of the cacao nibs and pat them into the sides, letting the excess fall to the counter. The cacao nibs will stick to the sides of the cheesecake. When finished going around, lightly pat the sides with your hand to embed the nibs even more. Garnish with tiny sprigs of fresh mint and serve!

Storage and life span: Cheesecakes will keep for at least four days. Store covered in the fridge.

Pecan Turtle Cheesecake

Makes one 10-inch cheesecake

CHOCOLATE-PECAN CRUST

1½ cups pecans
2 ounces cacao powder (weight)
⅓ cup cacao nibs
4 ounces date paste (weight)
⅛ teaspoon salt
1 teaspoon liquid vanilla

Process all ingredients. See cheesecake crust directions on page 82.

CARAMEL-CHOCOLATE FILLING

3 cups soaked cashews
¾ cup agave syrup
2 cups almond milk
2 tablespoons lemon juice
¼ teaspoon salt
¼ cup liquid vanilla
⅓ cup yacon syrup
3 tablespoons lecithin
1¼ cups coconut oil

Follow cheesecake filling directions on page 83. Reserve 2 cups of filling for swirling and add:

> 1½ ounces cacao powder (weight)
> 1 tablespoon liquid vanilla

Follow pouring/swirling directions on page 85.

Note: The swirl on top of this cheesecake will not be visible because it gets topped with caramel. The swirl here is for creating a marble effect on the inside of the cheesecake. Therefore it is not necessary to take the time to create a beautiful swirl on the top.

CARAMEL TOPPING
> ¾ cup macadamias (3½ ounces weight)
> 3 tablespoons agave syrup
> 1½ tablespoons liquid vanilla
> 2 tablespoons almond milk
> 2 tablespoons yacon syrup
> 3 tablespoons cacao butter
> ⅛ teaspoon salt

Blend all ingredients until smooth and creamy. Set in fridge to thicken, stirring often (15–20 minutes). Once caramel is thick but not hard, proceed to assembly directions below.

For the finishing of this cheesecake you will need the following:

> 1 cup pecans
> ⅛ teaspoon salt
> 2 tablespoons cacao nibs
> 1 tablespoon yacon syrup

Process the pecans and salt lightly so they are still mostly chunky.

FINISHING THE PECAN TURTLE CHEESECAKE
Start by taking ¾ cup of the processed pecans and applying them to the sides of the cheesecake. Do this by carefully holding the cheesecake from the bottom, over a counter. Take small handfuls of the

pecans and pat them into the sides, letting the excess fall to the counter. The pecans will stick to the sides of the cheesecake. When finished going around, lightly pat the sides with your hand to embed the pecans even more.

Now sprinkle 1 tablespoon of the cacao nibs and ¼ cup of the pecans evenly over the top. Gently spread the caramel on top of the cheesecake (over the nibs and pecans). Slowly and evenly drizzle the 1 tablespoon yacon syrup over the caramel, and lightly swirl with a chopstick. Finally, sprinkle the remaining pecans and cacao nibs over the top of the whole thing. Wow, what a cheesecake!

Pomegranate Cheesecake

Makes one 10-inch cheesecake

ALMOND CRUST
2 cups almonds
3 ounces date paste (weight)
¼ teaspoon liquid vanilla
⅛ teaspoon salt

Process all ingredients. See cheesecake crust directions on page 82.

POMEGRANATE FILLING
3 cups soaked cashews
2¼ cups pomegranate juice (see Chapter 1)
¼ cup lemon
¾ cup agave syrup
1 tablespoon liquid vanilla
¼ teaspoon salt
3 tablespoons lecithin
¾ cup coconut butter

Blend ingredients until smooth and creamy. Follow cheesecake filling directions on page 83. Garnish with pomegranate kernels and serve!

Pomegranate Cheesecake

Storage and life span: Cheesecakes will keep for at least four days. Store covered in the fridge.

Pumpkin–Chocolate Cheesecake

Makes a 10-inch cheesecake

CHOCOLATE-PECAN CRUST
1½ cups pecans
2 ounces cacao powder (weight)
⅓ cup cacao nibs
4 ounces date paste (weight)
⅛ teaspoon salt
1 tablespoon liquid vanilla

Process all ingredients. See cheesecake crust directions, page 82.

PUMPKIN-CHOCOLATE FILLING

3 cups soaked cashews

3 cups shredded butternut squash (7½ ounces weight)

1 cup almond milk

2 tablespoons lemon juice

1 cup agave syrup

¼ cup yacon syrup

2 tablespoons liquid vanilla

⅛ teaspoon salt

⅛ teaspoon turmeric

1 teaspoon cinnamon

¼ teaspoon nutmeg

3 tablespoons lecithin

1 cup coconut oil

Follow cheesecake filling directions on page 83. Reserve 2 cups of filling for swirling and add:

1 ounce cacao powder (weight)

1½ tablespoons liquid vanilla

Follow pouring/swirling directions on page 85.

Storage and life span: Cheesecakes will keep for at least four days. Store covered in the fridge.

Goji Berry–Chocolate Cheesecake

Makes one 10-inch cheesecake

CHOCOLATE-HEMPSEED CRUST

1¼ cups almonds

½ cup hempseeds

2 ounces cacao powder (weight)

4 ounces date paste (weight)

2 tablespoons liquid vanilla

⅛ teaspoon salt

Process all ingredients. See cheesecake crust directions on page 82.

GOJI BERRY–CHOCOLATE FILLING

2 cups goji berries (dry)
2 cups almond milk
2½ cups soaked cashews
½ cup agave syrup
¼ cup liquid vanilla
3 tablespoons lemon juice
¼ teaspoon salt
3 tablespoons lecithin
1¼ cup coconut oil

First soak the 2 cups goji berries with the 2 cups almond milk for about 2 hours. Once soaked, follow cheesecake filling directions on page 83.

Goji Berry–Chocolate Cheesecake

Reserve 2 cups of filling for swirling and add:

1 ounce cacao powder (weight)
2 tablespoons liquid vanilla

Follow pouring/swirling directions on page 85.

Storage and life span: Cheesecakes will keep for at least four days. Store covered in the fridge.

CHAPTER 5

Dehydration

We Are Worthy!

We are all completely worthy of the greatest life we can dream for ourselves. All we need is to accept this and truly believe how valuable we are. Our sense of worth directly reflects our self-esteem. Our beliefs about who we are, what is possible for ourselves, and what we are capable of create our sense of self-worth. We are the only ones responsible for our beliefs about our worth. Nothing external such as personal circumstances, other people's opinions, or a specific situation can define our self-worth. What we tell ourselves we are, we are. Our worth needs no evidence from our past or present achievements. Simply by existing we are worthy of everything life has to offer. We are all beautiful, magical, and creative beings who must constantly remind ourselves of our true nature.

Our worth is diminished every time we believe we are not good enough, smart enough, pretty enough, etc. At times we will dream about the day we will be "enough" and worthy of receiving everything we desire. At these times we forget that "someday" does not exist and will never exist until we make the decision that we are already good enough right now. Feeling worthy involves fully accepting ourselves the way we are and knowing that every aspect of ourselves is important. Positive affirmations are a useful tool for us to build and nourish our sense of worth. We are good enough right now!

Dehydrating food can sometimes seem like too long of a process to be worthwhile. We may feel intimidated or not so sure about dehydration. The incredible results from these recipes speak for themselves and are absolutely worth it! Dehydrating food for our purposes here means owning or having access to a thermostat-controlled dehydrator. These appliances gently blow hot air over food, causing it to lose its own moisture and dry out. This temperature-controlled process can take anywhere from hours to days, depending on what you are making. There are other creative ways to dehydrate food, using things like the sun, home-built systems, or ovens, but these recipes were formulated using a commercial dehydrator (Excalibur), and we do not recommend trying these recipes without the proper equipment. Dehydrating enables raw-food enthusiasts to attain a wider variety of ways they can eat their food. It creates endless possibilities with flavors, textures, and storage options. It's a very fun, creative, huge world once you start making things and experimenting.

Recipes

Equipment Needed

- Dehydrator
- Blender
- Food processor
- Mixer (only used in Brownie recipe)
- Measuring cups
- Measuring spoons
- Spatulas
- Cannoli forms (only for Cannoli recipe)
- Piping bag
- Coffee grinder
- Bowls

Dehydration Basics

Dehydrating is basically the raw way of "cooking" food. However, there is a big difference between dehydrating food and baking food, mainly degree of heat. To dehydrate something and have it still be considered raw, the food must never get above 115 degrees Fahrenheit. That's the food itself—the dehydrator may be set at a higher temperature than 115°, but that doesn't mean that the food is actually at that temperature. The proper way to dehydrate something is usually to "blast" the food with some air that is 145° for a short increment of time, then turn down the temperature to 115° for the rest of the dehydration time. This causes the food to "sweat" out quite a bit of moisture, which results in a quicker dehydration time and less chance of fermentation.

With most foods that get dehydrated, if the food is started at 115° and kept there the whole time, it may create a seal around the outside which holds the moisture in and could actually make the inside begin to ferment. This is not what you want to happen, and we can assure you that during the initial 145° segment the food itself does *not* get above 115°.

Keeping food below 115° is a fundamental rule with raw cuisine. When food is taken above that temperature enzymes die, vitamins are depleted, minerals are lost, and much more. Food that has been dehydrated should almost always be stored in an airtight container and not in the fridge. Putting dehydrated items in the fridge will cause them to absorb moisture and lose their dry texture.

Dehydrators come with sheets that are topped with a removable mesh sheet. They also come with a non-stick surface sheet that is used on top of the mesh sheet. These are called "teflex" sheets and are necessary in some recipes, whereas other recipes only require the mesh screen. Each recipe will specify whether or not you are supposed to use the teflex sheets.

Pecan Fudge Brownies

Makes about 20 servings

Step 1. Make Brazil nut milk (exact amount for making brownies):

>¾ cup Brazil nuts
>2 cups water

Blend until nuts are completely broken down. Allow to steep for 5 minutes, then strain milk. Reserve milked nut pulp (flour) for later in the recipe.

Step 2. In a blender, combine the following ingredients:

>1 cup Brazil nut milk
>1 cup soaked cashews
>½ cup cacao nibs
>⅓ cup agave syrup
>¼ cup liquid vanilla
>⅓ cup water

Blend until smooth. It may take several minutes for the cacao nibs to break down.

Step 3: In a mixer add the following ingredients:

>11 ounces date paste (weight)
>1½ ounces cacao powder (weight)
>1¼ teaspoons salt
>4 cups nut flour (any kind)

Mix on low speed (with paddle or whip attachment) until ingredients are well incorporated, then turn up speed and mix on medium/high for several minutes, or until all the date is broken down. Stop to add the reserved Brazil nut flour from Step 1 and the blended portion from Step 2. Resume mixing on low/medium until everything is consistent (3–5 minutes). Mixture should be fairly fluffy and soft. Transfer all of mixture onto one dehydrator sheet (no teflex) and gently spread evenly across the sheet.

Step 4. In a blender, combine the following ingredients:

> **The remaining Brazil nut milk (about 1¼ cups)**
> **½ cup cacao nibs**
> **4 tablespoons cacao powder**
> **½ cup agave syrup**
> **⅓ cup liquid vanilla**
> **¼ teaspoon salt**

Blend until thick and smooth. Pour directly on top of the brownie, which is spread out on the dehydrator sheet. Carefully spread it evenly over the batter, stopping about a half-inch from the edge so it doesn't ooze off.

Step 5. Top with:

> **½ cup pecans**

Sprinkle evenly over sheet, then lightly push them into the sauce with your hand or spatula.

Step 6. Dehydrate at 145° for 3 hours, then at 115° for 1–2 days, depending on how dry you want the final product. If you want the brownies pretty moist, only dehydrate for a full 24 hours. If you want them to be drier and chewier, dehydrate for two full days.

Also, if you want the brownies to be in nice squares, score them with a soft knife after the initial 3-hour dehydrating segment. If you don't care about the shape, the brownies will naturally crackle in a random way, which yields different-sized pieces. This recipe is ideal for making brownie chunks for use in a raw sundae.

Pecan Fudge Brownie Sundae with Chocolate and Caramel Sauces

Variations: Substitute other nuts for the Brazil nuts (for the milk) and the pecans. Any kind of nut flour will work, but Brazil and/or hazelnut flours produce a richer, more intense flavor.

Storage and life span: Store these brownies in an airtight container at room temperature.

The drier they are, the longer they will last, so anywhere from one to two weeks.

Shortbread Thumbprint Cookies with Goji Jam

Makes about 24 small cookies

SHORTBREAD COOKIE

2 cups soaked cashews

½ cup macadamias

1 cup dehydrated Brazil nut flour (see directions below)

½ cup agave syrup

2 tablespoons liquid vanilla

½ teaspoon salt

GOJI BERRY JAM

1¼ cups goji berries (dried)

7 tablespoons agave syrup

1½ teaspoons lemon juice

Small pinch salt

1 tablespoon water (or more, just enough to blend)

TO MAKE 1 CUP DEHYDRATED BRAZIL NUT FLOUR

Make Brazil nut milk by blending 1 cup Brazil nuts with 3 cups water. Strain out milk and set aside for other uses. Spread the nut pulp on a dehydrator sheet and dehydrate at 115° for 5–6 hours or until pulp is completely dry. Dehydrated nut flour will store in an airtight container kept at room temperature for many months.

Put Brazil nut flour in food processor and process until all chunks are broken down. Add the rest of the ingredients and process until smooth and the nuts have dissolved. Pipe or spoon little 1½-inch cookies onto a dehydrator sheet (no teflex).

Dehydrate at 145° for 3 hours, then turn down temperature to 115° and continue dehydrating for 2 days. After 2 days of dehydrating the cookies will be slightly dry, yet malleable. This is the perfect consistency to make the "thumbprint" indention and fill with the jam.

Make the Goji Jam by adding all ingredients except the water to the blender. While blending, slowly add just enough water to facilitate the process. The resulting jam should be thick.

Pull cookies out of dehydrator and make an indention with your finger in the middle of the cookie to create a dip. Make the dip fairly even and deep so the jam doesn't spill out. Spoon or pipe the jam into the dip, just enough to fill it.

Continue to dehydrate at 115° for another 1–2 days, or until the cookies easily come off the dehydrator mesh sheet (also depends upon how dry you want it).

Storage and life span: Keep in an airtight container at room temperature. Try to avoid stacking these cookies or the goji jam will get messy. They will last one to two weeks.

Shortbread Thumbprint Cookies with Goji Jam and Lemon-Cashew Cookies

Lemon–Cashew Cookies

Makes about 25 small cookies

2 cups soaked cashews
¾ cup agave syrup
½ cup lemon juice
1 cup coconut flakes
¼ teaspoon salt
½ tablespoon liquid vanilla

Put all ingredients in food processor and process until consistency is like thick oatmeal (1–2 minutes), stopping to scrape down sides of processor bowl as needed. Spoon or pipe small 1½ inch cookies onto dehydrator sheet (no teflex).

Dehydrate at 145° for 3 hours, then turn down to 115°. Dehydrate at 115° for 2–3 days, or until cookies are dry but still chewy. Cookies should be easy to remove from mesh sheet.

Variations: You can substitute other citrus juices for the lemon. Try lime, orange, Meyer lemon, grapefruit, or combinations thereof.

Storage and life span: Store in an airtight container at room temperature. Cookies will last two to three weeks.

Chocolate Chunk Walnut Cookies

Makes about 16 large cookies

4 cups almond flour

¾ cup flax meal (powder half-cup whole flax seeds in coffee
   grinder)

2 teaspoons salt

½ cup liquid vanilla

1¼ cups agave syrup

1½ cups fudge chunks (Raw Cacao Fudge recipe, page 162)

1½ cups walnuts (preferably walnut halves or large pieces)

Combine all ingredients except fudge and walnuts in bowl. Mix
together until thoroughly combined. Mixture should hold together
and not be too wet.

Take some pieces of already prepared Raw Cacao Fudge and
break up by hand or with knife into small to medium-sized chunks.
Combine the fudge and walnuts with the dough and evenly mix in.

Form the dough into a log, roughly 3 inches in diameter, and cut
half-inch slices. Form slices into cookie shapes by hand and lay on
dehydrator sheet (no teflex).

Dehydrate at 145° for 3 hours, then at 115° for 24 hours. Cookies should be slightly moist on the inside.

Variations: You can replace the walnuts with any other kind of nut.
The flour can also be any kind of nut flour. The fudge can be substituted with whole cacao beans, but the fudge and the way it dehy-
drates is really what makes this cookie amazing.

Storage and life span: Store in an airtight container at room temperature. Cookies should last one to two weeks.

Chocolate Chunk Walnut Cookies (top) and Ginger Spice–Cranberry Cookies

Ginger Spice-Cranberry Cookies

Makes 20 large cookies

4 cups almond flour

¾ cup flax meal (powder ½ cup whole flax seeds
   in coffee grinder)

½ cup date paste (6 ounces weight)

2 cups pecans

½ cup yacon syrup

½ cup agave syrup

¼ cup ginger juice

¼ cup liquid vanilla

2 teaspoons salt

2 tablespoons cinnamon

½ teaspoon nutmeg

½ teaspoon cardamom

¼ teaspoon clove

1½ cups cranberries (dried)

Combine the flour, flax meal, vanilla, and ginger juice in a bowl and mix until well incorporated.

In a food processor, process pecans briefly with salt and spices, then add date paste and continue processing until everything is well broken down and has a crust-like consistency.

Combine everything from the mixture above with the rest of the ingredients. Mix by hand until all ingredients are well combined. Form into a log shape about three inches in diameter. Cut half-inch slices and form into cookie shapes. Place cookies on a dehydrator sheet (no teflex).

Dehydrate at 145° for 3 hours, then turn down to 115° and continue dehydrating for another 24 hours. Cookies should still be slightly moist on the inside.

Variations: You can replace the cranberries with any kind of dried berry or fruit, such as goji berries, mulberries, or raisins. Walnuts can be substituted for the pecans.

Storage and life span: Store in an airtight container at room temperature. These cookies should last one to two weeks.

Cashew Crêpes with Berry Jam
Makes 4 large crêpes

CASHEW CRÊPE
1½ cups soaked cashews
2 tablespoons lemon juice
¼ teaspoon salt
¼ cup agave syrup
½ cup water

BERRY JAM
1 cup blueberries
1 tablespoon + 1 teaspoon lemon juice
small pinch salt
2 teaspoons liquid vanilla
6 tablespoons date paste
2 cups chopped strawberries

CASHEW CRÈME FRAICHE
1½ cups soaked cashews
¼ cup lemon juice
2 tablespoons agave syrup
small pinch salt
1 teaspoon liquid vanilla
¾ cup water

MAKING THE CRÊPE
Blend all crêpe ingredients until smooth and consistent. Pour out onto a dehydrator sheet (with teflex) and spread with a spatula until mixture forms an even, thin layer. (It should cover the entire dehydrator sheet, leaving a half-inch border.) Dehydrate at 145° for 1

hour, then turn down temperature to 115° and continue dehydrating for another 18 hours. The mixture should not be fully dry, just soft and pliable enough to roll.

With a butter knife (or some similar non-sharp object), gently cut through the dehydrated crêpe to create four equal-sized crêpes. These are now ready to use. Simply fill with the berry jam, roll up, top with crème fraiche, and serve.

Serving tip: Sprinkle some whole berries on top before serving.

MAKING THE BERRY JAM

Blend all ingredients except the strawberries until smooth. Don't over-blend as this may cause the jam to lose color.

Pour blended mixture into a small bowl and toss in the chopped strawberries. Stir them in until mixture is consistent.

Cashew Crêpe with Berry Jam

MAKING THE CRÈME FRAICHE

Blend all ingredients until smooth and creamy.

Pour directly from blender onto finished, rolled crêpes. You can also transfer the crème fraiche to a squeeze bottle for easier use.

Variations: The blueberries in the jam can be replaced with any kind of fresh berry. The real variation with these crêpes comes with the filling. You can put just about anything you wish in these crêpes, sweet or savory. One truly amazing variation is to fill the crêpe with sliced banana, Macadamia Caramel sauce (recipe on page 127), and our Raw Chocolate Sauce (recipe on page 161). Decorate top of crêpe with more of both sauces. Wow!

Note: Once filled, serve crêpes immediately, as they will start to absorb moisture and after about an hour will lose their texture and definition.

Storage and life span: The crêpes will last for at least a week but should ideally be eaten shortly after they are ready. Store unused crêpes in an airtight container at room temperature. The jam and the crème fraiche will both last about four to five days.

Pistachio Baklava

Makes 12 servings

BAKLAVA "PHYLLO DOUGH"
1½ cups soaked cashews
2 tablespoons lemon juice
¼ teaspoon salt
2 tablespoons agave syrup
½ cup water
1 tablespoon liquid vanilla

Blend all ingredients until smooth and creamy; you will need a blender plunger for this. Pour on dehydrator sheet (with teflex) and carefully spread around with a spatula until mixture is covering most of the sheet in a thin, consistent layer. Dehydrate at 145° for 1 hour, then at 115° for a full 24 hours. Sheet should not be fully dry—you want to be able to pick it up and work with it, not have it crumble apart.

PISTACHIO SPICE FILLING
1½ cups pistachios
¼ teaspoon salt
4 tablespoons agave syrup
½ tablespoon liquid vanilla
½ tablespoon lemon juice
¼ teaspoon clove
¼ teaspoon cardamom

Lightly process the pistachios, salt, and spices first. Add the rest of the ingredients and continue processing until mixture is consistent and pistachios are still slightly chunky.

BAKLAVA ASSEMBLY DIRECTIONS
Carefully cut the dehydrated "phyllo dough" into four equal-size pieces, and then divide the Pistachio Spice Filling into three equal-size portions. Put one piece of dough down as the bottom layer, and

then gently spread (by hand is easiest) one portion of the filling evenly on top of the bottom layer. Gently place another layer of dough on top, and continue alternating until there are four total layers of dehydrated dough and three layers of Pistachio Spice Filling. Now, with a sharp serrated knife, carefully cut into 12 equal-size pieces.

TOPPING

1–2 tablespoons yacon syrup

Lightly drizzle a small amount of the yacon syrup on top of each serving. Using a brush or your finger, spread syrup evenly to create a light-brown "glaze."

Storage and life span: This baklava should last for at least one week. Store in an airtight container at room temperature.

Pistachio Baklava

Cinnamon Buns
with Macadamia Caramel

Makes 6 buns

CINNAMON DOUGH

½ cup soaked almonds
2 cups almond flour
½ cup flax seed (powdered in coffee grinder)
5 ounces date paste (weight)
2 teaspoons liquid vanilla
1 teaspoon cinnamon
1 teaspoon salt
¾ cup coconut milk

Coarsely chop the soaked almonds by hand. Add all ingredients except coconut milk to mixer bowl. Mix on low/medium speed until date paste has broken down. Now add coconut milk a little at a time until you have a consistency somewhat like bread dough. The entire amount of coconut milk may not be necessary to achieve this effect. Dough should be wet enough to stick together, but not soupy or runny.

FILLING/TOPPING

2 cups pecans
½ cup agave syrup
2 teaspoons cinnamon
¼ teaspoon salt
¼ teaspoon liquid vanilla

Combine all ingredients in bowl and stir until well mixed.

MACADAMIA CARAMEL

1 cup macadamias
¼ teaspoon salt
¼ cup almond milk
½ cup agave syrup

Cinnamon Bun with Macadamia Caramel

     1 teaspoon liquid vanilla
     1 tablespoon yacon syrup

Blend all ingredients until smooth and creamy. Make caramel right before you are ready to serve the cinnamon buns.

ASSEMBLING AND DEHYDRATING THE BUNS
Once the dough is ready, spread it out on a teflex sheet to about a half-inch thickness. Reserve half the amount of filling to top buns. Spread the remaining filling evenly on the dough, leaving 2 inches of space on one side to facilitate rolling and prevent the filling from spilling out.

Start rolling from the side that is opposite the part with extra space, and roll dough into a round log. Keep your hands moist to prevent sticking. Seal the edge by smoothing over the dough. Slice the log into 6 equal-size pieces, which should be about ¾–1 inch thick. Place buns on a dehydrator sheet (with teflex). Evenly distribute the reserved pecan filling on top of each bun. Dehydrate for 2 hours at 145° then turn down to 115° and continue dehydrating overnight. Top with Macadamia Caramel before serving.

Note: Buns are best when they are served warm, right out of the dehydrator.

Storage and life span: These rolls should last for at least three days and can be stored in an airtight container at room temperature.

Raw Buckwheat Granola
Makes about 10 cups

1½ cups soaked almonds
1½ cups soaked whole buckwheat
5 cups coarsely chopped apples (about 7 small apples)
10 ounces date paste (weight)
¼ cup dried cranberries
2½ cups coconut flakes
¾ cup agave syrup
¼ cup liquid vanilla
2 teaspoons cinnamon
½ teaspoon salt

Soak buckwheat 6–8 hours. Drain and rinse well. Place all ingredients in a mixer bowl and mix on low/medium speed until date paste is broken down and all ingredients are thoroughly combined.

Distribute the granola in an even layer among three dehydrator sheets (with teflex). Dehydrate for 1 hour at 145°, then turn down temperature to 115° and continue dehydrating overnight, or until granola is dry enough to peel off the teflex sheets. Transfer to dehydrator sheets without teflex and continue dehydrating at 115° until dry (about 2 full days).

Variations: You can create endless variations of this granola using your own creativity and the flavors you love. Try using pear instead of apple, any other kind of dried fruit for the cranberries, or experiment with different seeds.

Storage and life span: Fully dry granola will keep for several weeks. Store in an airtight container at room temperature.

Cannoli

Makes 12 cannoli

SPECIAL EQUIPMENT:
12 cannoli forms

CANNOLI SHELL
1½ cups soaked cashews
½ cup water
¼ cup agave syrup
3 tablespoons liquid vanilla
2½ tablespoons lemon juice
2 tablespoons flax seeds (processed in coffee grinder)
⅛ teaspoon salt

Finely powder the flax seeds using a coffee grinder. Soak the flax seed powder with a half-cup water for 5 minutes (or until mixture has a jelly-like consistency).

Add to blender soaked cashews, flax mixture, agave, liquid vanilla, lemon juice, and salt. Blend really well until the mixture is

Cannoli

smooth and creamy. Pour out onto a dehydrator sheet (with teflex) and spread with a spatula until mixture forms an even, thin layer. It should cover the entire dehydrator sheet, leaving a half-inch border.

Start dehydrating at 145° for 1 hour then reduce temperature to 115°. Dehydrate for 24 hours or until the shell dough is dry enough to hold together but still flexible.

Cut the shell dough lengthwise into twelve one-inch wide strips. Roll each strip around cannoli form, overlapping by a half-inch as you roll. If the dough is too dry and begins to crack, rub a small amount of water with your finger on dough strip to soften. Be gentle since the dough is still fragile. Place each rolled cannoli on a dehydrator sheet (with teflex).

Once all the strips are rolled around the forms, dehydrate at 115° for another 24 hours or until the shell is dry and crunchy. Gently slide cannoli shell off the form. Set the shells aside at room temperature.

CANNOLI FILLING
1½ cups soaked cashews
½ cup agave syrup
¾ cup coconut milk
¼ cup lemon juice
4 tablespoons vanilla
⅛ teaspoon turmeric
⅛ teaspoon salt
1 tablespoon lecithin
½ cup + 2 tablespoons coconut oil

Add to blender all ingredients except the coconut oil and lecithin. Blend well until smooth and creamy (3–5 minutes). Stop blending and add the lecithin and melted coconut oil. Resume blending until oil and lecithin are well incorporated.

Set in the freezer for 1–2 hours or until the filling is firm.

Fill a pastry bag with cannoli filling and pipe the filling into each shell. Serve immediately.

Storage and life span: Cannoli shells will hold fine at room temperature in an airtight container for one to two weeks. The filling will last in the fridge for at least four days.

Always fill the cannoli shell right before serving, as the filling will soften the shells.

Chocolate Soufflé

Makes twelve 4-ounce soufflé cups

1 cup Brazil nut flour
1 cup soaked cashews
1 cup agave syrup
3 ounces cacao powder (weight)
2 tablespoons liquid vanilla
½ teaspoon salt
½ cup Brazil nut milk
1 cup macadamias

Thank you to Arielle Webb for this fantastic recipe!

Place all ingredients except Brazil nut milk and macadamias in food processor and process well until smooth and creamy.

Blend the Brazil nut milk and macadamias in blender until smooth and macadamias have dissolved.

Add blended portion to food processor and process all ingredients together until smooth and consistent.

Using a spoon or ice cream scoop, distribute mixture evenly among 12 small cups, about 4 ounces' capacity (ideally use small ramekins). Dehydrate cups at 145° for 3 hours. Lower the temperature to 115° and keep dehydrating for 2 full days. Finished soufflé should be slightly dry to the touch on the top, and moist and warm on the inside. Best served warm with some raw ice cream!

Variation: You can use a 1½ inch-diameter (small) ice cream scoop to create Chocolate Soufflé cookies. Instead of filling cups, scoop soufflé mixture onto a dehydrator sheet (with teflex). Form small egg-shaped cookies so that there is an inner portion which remains soft and moist. Dehydrate at 145° for 3 hours and then lower the temperature to 115° and dehydrate for 3 full days.

Storage and life span: Chocolate Soufflé in the cup will keep for at least three days in an airtight container at room temperature. The cookies should last for at least two weeks. Keep cookies in an airtight container at room temperature.

Vanilla, Mint-Chip,
and Chocolate Ice Creams

CHAPTER 6

Ice Cream

Forgiveness

To forgive is to accept our own or someone else's mistakes. Forgiveness is a conscious choice we make. It doesn't just happen by itself or occur because we have forgotten. Forgiveness is not based on who is right or wrong; it is based on the acceptance of others, the world, and ourselves. True forgiveness comes from a place of unconditional love. We all make mistakes. What's important is to learn from those mistakes and to celebrate them as we learn infinitely more from our failures than we do from our successes. There is always an opportunity for our personal growth when we make a mistake, if we are first willing to forgive ourselves.

Continually holding a grudge towards others or ourselves only prevents us from moving forward. Staying focused on the mistake instead of acknowledging the lesson simply makes the mistake seem bigger and harder to resolve. Withholding forgiveness weighs us down and often results in feelings of stress, anger, and disillusionment—to name just a few. When we choose to forgive, we experience liberation from negative emotions and can leave the past behind. Forgiving gives us a fresh start, a freedom to truly enjoy the present moment.

When we don't live up to our expectations or fulfill our high standards, we must learn to always forgive ourselves and put our attention on things we are proud of. Any step, however small it may seem, taken in the direction of your health is actually a big step. Be proud of them!

If you make a mistake with these recipes, forgive yourself. Sometimes a mistake can lead to the creation of a new incredible recipe!

These delicious ice creams are a special treat for any occasion. All of the recipes require a hand-cranked ice cream maker. (They will also work with a professional automatic ice cream maker.) This tool is easy to find and is a fun way to enjoy your own homemade ice cream. The base of our raw ice creams is always nuts or coconut, and they are sweetened with agave (you can also sweeten with dates, the ice cream just won't come out as smooth). These ice cream recipes are wonderful combined with pie, cobbler, cake, and even many of our dehydrated items. By themselves, these decadent ice creams are the perfect refreshing dessert. One of the best uses of these ice creams is for the creation of a variety of amazing milkshakes!

Recipes

Equipment Needed

- Blender
- Hand-cranked ice cream maker
- Measuring cups
- Measuring spoons
- Spatulas
- Rolling pin
- Ice cream scoop
- Cookie cutter (3-inch diameter)

Hand-Cranked Ice Cream Directions

Blend all the ingredients really well until they are completely broken down. When ready, place mixture in an airtight container in the fridge for a few hours. A cold ice cream mixture will more readily freeze into ice cream. Make sure the inside cylinder part of the hand-cranked ice cream maker is really frozen. Ideally you want to have this part in the freezer always ready to go.

Assemble the hand-cranked ice cream maker. (Set the frozen cylinder inside the container.)

Pour ice cream mixture into the hand-cranked ice cream maker and crank handle continuously until desired consistency is achieved. Ingredients that you want to remain chunky can be added at this point (such as coconut flakes).

This ice cream is great by itself or with a variety of toppings such as Raw Chocolate Sauce (see page 161), fresh berries, chunks of Raw Cacao Fudge (see page 162), Caramel Sauce (see page 127), or cacao nibs and or your choice of chopped nuts sprinkled on top.

If you are making ice cream sandwiches or milkshakes, transfer finished ice cream to a container and put in freezer until ready to use.

Storage and life span: This kind of ice cream is best eaten right away, as freezing it will make the ice cream hard. If you do choose to store ice cream, keep in freezer in an airtight container. Frozen ice cream should keep for at least one month.

Coconut Ice Cream

Makes about 4 servings

1½ cups coconut milk
½ cup coconut meat (wet measurement)
¼ cup + 2 tablespoons agave syrup
½ cup coconut flakes
1 tablespoon vanilla
¼ + ⅛ teaspoon salt
1 tablespoon lecithin

Blend all ingredients really well. Follow hand-cranked ice cream directions (see page 138). Add to ice cream maker before cranking:

> ¼ cup coconut flakes (in addition to the ½ cup already blended)

Vanilla Ice Cream

Makes about 4 servings

1 cup almond milk
1 cup soaked cashews
¼ cup + 2 tablespoons agave syrup
1 vanilla bean (scraped insides only)
¼ cup liquid vanilla
1 tablespoon lecithin
¼ + ⅛ teaspoon salt

Blend all ingredients really well. Follow hand-cranked ice cream directions (see page 138).

Variations: This basic vanilla ice cream can be varied in many ways by adding extra flavors. Our favorite variation is Mint-Chip Ice Cream. To make this flavor simply blend into the basic recipe 1 bunch of fresh spearmint (leaves only). Then add 3 tablespoons cacao nibs directly into the ice cream maker before cranking.

Butter Pecan Ice Cream

Makes about 4 servings

1½ cups water
½ cup pecans
½ cup macadamias
2 tablespoons liquid vanilla
¼ cup agave syrup

1 tablespoon lecithin
¼ + ⅛ teaspoon salt
2 teaspoons yacon syrup

Blend all ingredients really well. Follow hand-cranked ice cream directions (see page 138).

Chocolate Ice Cream

Makes about 4 servings

1¼ cups hazelnut milk
1 cup soaked cashews
½ cup agave syrup
5 tablespoons cacao powder
2 tablespoons vanilla
1 tablespoon lecithin
¼ + ⅛ teaspoon salt

Blend all ingredients really well. Follow hand-cranked ice cream directions (see page 138).

Brazil Nut Ice Cream

Makes about 4 servings

1¼ cups Brazil nut milk
¾ cup soaked cashews
2 tablespoons vanilla
¼ cup agave syrup
1 tablespoon lecithin
¼ + ⅛ teaspoon salt

Blend all ingredients really well. Follow hand-cranked ice cream directions (see page 138).

Ice Cream Sandwich Directions

Add to food processor the nuts, salt, vanilla, half the amount of date paste, and any other ingredients the recipe may call for.

Process all ingredients until mixture starts to rise on the sides of the processor bowl. Stop the machine and mix with a spatula or spoon.

Repeat a few times until nuts are well broken down. Add remaining date paste and continue processing until mixture is consistent. The final result of the cookie "dough" should be a mixture that can hold together with a gentle pressure and be broken apart with a clean break. Cookie dough should not be too sticky, so pay attention to how wet your date paste is. The entire portion of date paste called for may not be necessary if the paste is overly moist.

Before rolling out the cookies, you first need to finely process a half-cup of almonds to a flour-like consistency. This is used to prevent the cookies from sticking to the rolling pin and cutting board. Using a rolling pin, roll out cookie dough into an even layer, about ⅛ inch thick. Using a 3-inch-diameter round cookie cutter, cut out the cookies. Freeze cookies for several hours before assembling sandwiches.

Using whatever type of ice cream you wish (pages 138–140) scoop a medium-sized ball of firm ice cream on top of one cookie. Place another cookie on the other side and gently press sandwich together. Freeze entire sandwich briefly before serving (ice cream should not be melting). A nice addition is to halfway dip sandwich in melted chocolate (recipe, page 160). Make sure sandwiches are well frozen before dipping.

Vanilla Ice Cream Sandwiches

Makes 8 sandwiches (16 cookies)

VANILLA COOKIE

2 cups almonds (+ ½ cup additional for rolling)
½ teaspoon salt
1½ tablespoons liquid vanilla
4 ounces (weight) date paste (about ⅓ cup)

Process all ingredients. See ice cream sandwich directions, page 141.

Storage and life span: Always keep ice cream sandwiches in the freezer in an airtight container. If properly stored, sandwiches will keep for at least one month.

Chocolate Ice Cream Sandwiches

Makes 8 sandwiches (16 cookies)

CHOCOLATE COOKIE

1¾ cups almonds
½ teaspoon salt
5 ounces date paste (weight)
3 ounces cacao powder (weight)
2 tablespoons liquid vanilla

Process all ingredients. See ice cream sandwich directions, page 141.

Storage and life span: Always keep ice cream sandwiches in the freezer in an airtight container. If properly stored, sandwiches will keep for at least one month.

Ice Cream Sandwiches

Ginger Spice Ice Cream Sandwiches

Makes 8 sandwiches (16 cookies)

GINGER SPICE COOKIE
1¾ cups almonds
½ teaspoon salt
1 teaspoon cinnamon
⅛ teaspoon nutmeg
⅛ teaspoon clove
2 tablespoons freshly grated ginger
3 ounces date paste (weight)
1 teaspoon liquid vanilla

Process all ingredients. See ice cream sandwich directions, page 141.

Storage and life span: Always keep ice cream sandwiches in the freezer in an airtight container. If properly stored, sandwiches will keep for at least one month.

Milkshake Directions

Start by making ice cream of your choice and freezing it until firm. Completely frozen ice cream may need to be slightly thawed before using.

Blend all ingredients in recipe except the ice cream until thoroughly combined.

Stop blending, add the ice cream, and briefly pulse-blend until ice cream is incorporated. Over-blending will melt the ice cream and reduce the milkshake's thickness. Serve immediately and enjoy!

Vanilla Milkshake

Makes one large milkshake (about 2 cups volume)

1 cup Vanilla Ice Cream (recipe, page 139)
¾ cup almond milk
2 large pitted dates
small pinch salt
1 tablespoon liquid vanilla

Follow milkshake directions, above.

Variation: For a chocolate milkshake simply blend in 1 tablespoon cacao powder. You can also add your favorite powdered superfood, such as maca, açaí, or green food.

Mint-Chip Milkshake

Makes one large milkshake (about 2 cups volume)

1 cup Vanilla Ice Cream (recipe, page 139)
¾ cup almond milk
2 large pitted dates
15 large mint leaves
1 tablespoon cacao nibs
1 teaspoon green food (we use Vitamineral Green by
    HealthForce Nutritionals)
small pinch salt
½ tablespoon liquid vanilla

Follow milkshake directions, page 144.

Orange Dream Milkshake

Makes one large milkshake (about 2 cups volume)

1 cup Vanilla Ice Cream (recipe, page 139)
¾ cup orange juice
1 tablespoon liquid vanilla
small pinch salt

Follow milkshake directions, page 144.

Espresso Milkshake

Makes one large milkshake (about 2 cups volume)

1 cup Vanilla Ice Cream (recipe, page 139)
6 tablespoons cold-pressed espresso
6 tablespoons almond milk
2 large pitted dates
small pinch salt
½ tablespoon liquid vanilla

Follow milkshake directions, page 144.

Almond Butter–Cacao Nib Milkshake

Makes one large milkshake (about 2 cups volume)

1 cup Vanilla Ice Cream (recipe, page 139)
⅔ cup almond milk
3 tablespoons almond butter
2 large pitted dates
1 tablespoon cacao nibs
small pinch salt
½ tablespoon liquid vanilla

Follow milkshake directions, page 144.

CHAPTER 7

Cacao

Love

Love is the most powerful force in the Universe. It is all-embracing, unlimited, unconditional, and endless. Love is the energy that overcomes all obstacles. It is the universal language that everyone understands. It is our instinct to love and be loved.

It all starts with us. Before we can give or receive love, we must first love ourselves. To love ourselves means to fully accept how beautiful we are, to celebrate our talents, honor our bodies, and to cherish our unique personalities. When we love ourselves we experience inner peace, mental clarity, strength, confidence, and joy.

Love is the ultimate goal of our human experience. We are here to learn how to give and receive love by practicing "being" love. To be love is to be an expression of love in everything we do, say, and think. When something is not an expression of love it is an expression of fear. Whenever we are confronted with fear within ourselves or from others we must remember that it is simply a call for love, and the answer is to give love. We all want to experience love and sometimes look for it from an outside source when we are the source. The love we all long for is inside each one of us, and our challenge is to recognize this. Once we acknowledge this we will be able to project love all around us, and the world will generously reflect this love back.

Food is the physical manifestation of the Earth's love for us. Preparing and sharing food are some of the ways we give love to others. We practice "being love" when preparing our food. Our energy is directly infused into everything we create, including the food that we make.

Chocolate has been enjoyed for thousands of years as a way of connecting with the divine love of the Universe. No food symbolizes love better than chocolate. We would like to reveal the ancient mystery we have uncovered, learned after years of searching: the secret ingredient in every recipe is Love!

Raw cacao (kuh-cow) is the real, unadulterated, whole-food source of chocolate. It is the original and the best. And the best for you too: raw cacao is one of the world's most amazing superfoods, bursting with copious amounts of vitamins, minerals, antioxidants, and "happy brain" chemicals! The chocolate tree, botanically known as *Theobroma cacao,* is a tropical tree that can get quite tall and produces large pod-like fruits, the seeds of which are the source of everybody's beloved chocolate. Unrefined and unprocessed, cacao is the "Food of the Gods" (*Theobroma cacao*'s literal translation).

Chocolate in its natural state is a totally guilt-free, nourishing, wonderful, heart-opening food! Over the history of human consumption of cacao, it has been used to treat a variety of physical ailments while also acting as an aphrodisiac and an anti-depressant; and it was even used as currency in ancient Central American cultures. Cacao is an extremely complex, unique, and magical substance containing more than two thousand different chemical compounds, many of which we know about, yet there continues to be mystery surrounding what is in cacao and what it can do.

We only use the raw versions of cacao products for our chocolate desserts and candies: cacao powder, cacao butter, cacao nibs, and whole beans. This chapter is full of cacao delicacies, which are not only delicious but offer a huge amount of nutritional benefits. Enjoy!

Recipes

Equipment Needed

- Blender
- Food processor
- Measuring cups
- Measuring spoons
- Spatulas
- Bowls
- Ice cream/Truffle scoops
- Chocolate molds/Mini baking cups
- Square pan, 8x8x2 inch
- Heavy waxed paper or teflex sheet

About *Theobroma Cacao*

Swedish scientist Carl von Linnaeus officially named the chocolate tree *Theobroma cacao* back in 1753. Literally translated "cacao, food of the gods," he named the genus exactly what the native Central Americans called it.

Cacao trees thrive best in tropical/subtropical climates and can grow anywhere from 10–30 feet high when mature. The tree flowers and produces fruit all year. The flowers/fruit grow straight out of the trunk and large branches. Once pollinated, the flower develops into a pod-like green fruit that matures into the characteristic red, orange, yellow, and even blue and purple pods, depending on the variety. It takes 5–6 months for the pod to ripen. The ripe pod is about 18–20 centimeters long and contains 20–50 almond-like seeds surrounded by a sweet white pulp. These seeds are the cacao "beans." Cacao is indigenous to Central/South America but now grows in most tropical climates in the 20-degree latitude zone around the world. Cacao will grow on its own but thrives best under a canopy of other mixed trees (in partial shade) in a jungle type of ecosystem.

Main Varieties of Cacao

The three major varieties of cacao that are heavily cultivated are called Criollo, Forastero, and Trinitario. The Criollo cacao pods are longer and deeply ridged, and are red/yellow but sometimes blue/purple. Criollo is prized for its amazingly rich, pronounced flavor and aromatic nuances. Compared to other varieties, Criollo is prone to disease, ripens late, and has small harvests, which accounts for why this variety makes up only 5% of the world cacao crop. Because of its lower productivity, Criollo is used only in very high-end chocolates since it has the best flavor. Criollo is mainly grown in Venezuela, Ecuador, and Colombia.

Forastero was cultivated later than Criollo, and it has fruit pods that are yellow/orange, rounder, and less ridged than Criollo pods. Forastero cacaos are more vigorous, hardy trees that are very disease-resistant. Originally from the Amazon basin, they are mainly cultivated in Africa and Asia today, comprising 80% of the world's crop. The flavor of Forastero beans is less refined and complex than Criollo, but the plant is so much easier to grow.

Trinitario is the natural hybrid of the Criollo and Forastero subspecies and was domesticated in the late eighteenth century. Trinitario is the best of both worlds; it has the rich flavor and complexity of Criollo and the robust strength of Forastero. Trinitario is mainly cultivated in South America and the West Indies and accounts for 15% of the world cacao harvest.

Cacao vs. Cocoa

A slight changing of letters represents a very major difference. "Cocoa" was the British term for cacao. The current association with the word "cocoa" is the defatted, alkalized powder form of chocolate invented by the Dutchman Coenraad Van Houten in 1828.

As early as 1815 in his Amsterdam factory, Van Houten had been developing a very efficient hydraulic press that squeezed the oil out of cacao. This new process reduced the fat content of cacao to 27% (from 50–55%), and primed it to become ground into powder. He eventually treated his cocoa powder with alkaline salts (potassium or sodium carbonates) in order to have the powder dissolve well in water. Van Houten created what would eventually be called "cocoa" or "cocoa powder." This processing of chocolate became known as "Dutching," which "cooked" the chocolate, giving it a darker color and a diluted flavor. Dutching made it possible to create large-scale manufacturing and distribution of cheap chocolate, eventually available to millions of people worldwide in powdered and solid forms.

The nutritional value of cacao was further lessened when "milk chocolate" was invented due to the efforts of two Swiss men: chemist Henri Nestle and chocolate producer Daniel Peter. In 1867, Nestle developed a process to powder milk via evaporation. This single discovery has led to Nestle becoming the largest food corporation in the world. Then, in 1879, the first milk chocolate bar was produced after Daniel Peter experimented with adding the milk powder to chocolate. Although generally praised as a great milestone in the evolution of chocolate, it was this addition of powdered milk that blocked the body's absorption of the healing nutrients of cacao. The occasional person who thinks that they have an "allergy" to chocolate is, with the ultra-rare exception, usually allergic to the pasteurized dairy, refined sugar, or caffeine that is in most chocolate. We have personally met people who considered themselves allergic and had them try raw cacao without any problems.

Benefits of Raw Cacao

Magnesium: This is one of the most essential minerals, yet studies say that more than 80% of the United States' population is deficient in magnesium. In nature, the most concentrated source of magnesium is raw cacao! Other good sources of the mineral include certain nuts and any chlorophyll-rich green veggies. Magnesium is found at the center of the chlorophyll molecule. Magnesium supports the heart, increases brainpower, relaxes the muscles, increases flexibility, causes healthy bowel movements, and helps build strong bones. As one of the body's primary alkaline minerals, magnesium assists the normal functioning of several chemical enzymatic processes—facilitating more than three hundred different detoxification and elimination functions.

Chromium: This mineral helps balance blood sugar levels, and cacao has ten times the amount of chromium as whole wheat, a chromium-rich food, making it the highest food source of this mineral.

Antioxidant Power: Raw cacao beans are super-rich in antioxidant flavonols. They contain 10,000 mg (10 grams) of flavonol antioxidants (that's a 10% antioxidant concentration level!). This makes cacao possibly the best source of antioxidants, with twenty to thirty times more than red wine or green tea.

Vitamins B1, B2, B5, B6, C, and E are all present in significant quantities.

Other Nutrients: Fiber, iron, niacin, phosphorus, as well as hundreds of other chemicals and phytonutients (special plant nutrients) are found in cacao.

As stated earlier, cacao is highly complex in its structure, and not all its constituents have even been identified yet. It is clear that there are very special and unique properties in cacao, especially in relation to human brain chemistry. Below are listed the four main chemicals that are found in high amounts in cacao and certainly produce noticeable effects.

The "Happy Brain" Chemicals

Theobromine: The base chemical theobromine is sparsely distributed in the plant kingdom, occurring in only nineteen known species, but you may have heard of these other popular theobromine-containing substances: coffee, tea, yerba maté, and the kola nut. Yes, theobromine is the sister molecule to caffeine; however, it is much milder and has only about a quarter of the stimulating power that caffeine has. Theobromine dilates blood vessels, has proven to be an effective cough remedy, and has shown cariostatic effects (it destroys the bacteria that cause tooth decay). Depending on the study, caffeine has been found in low amounts, or not at all, in the cacao bean (or in the shell and not in the bean). This inconsistency is considered to be the result of confusion between the two very similar molecules, theobromine and caffeine. One thing is for sure, cooked chocolate definitely has caffeine, a result of the chemical transformation of theobromine to caffeine when it is exposed to heat.

Phenylethylamine (fennel-ethel-uh-mean) or PEA: This is sometimes called the "love" or "happy" chemical. The brain releases PEA naturally when we are really excited, happy, or sexually aroused. PEA is the structural molecule behind catecholamine neurotransmitters (brain chemicals) in parts of the brain that control our ability to pay attention and stay alert. When the brain is flooded with PEA, different chemical reactions take place that make one excitable, joyous, and focused! So our brains naturally produce this wonderful chemical, but it is also found pre-made by nature in (only) two amazingly synergistic raw foods: raw cacao and blue-green algae.

Anandamide (uh-non-da-mide): This neurotransmitter known as the "bliss" chemical is an endogenous cannabinoid naturally found in the human brain. It is a type of brain lipid (oil) that is released when we are feeling really good. The name is derived from the Sanskrit word "ananda," meaning bliss. Cacao and cannabis (marijuana) are the only plants known to contain cannabinoids, chemicals that lock onto certain receptor sites in the brain in a "lock & key" system. The result is the feeling of being elated or high.

The chemical our body produces that normally fills the cannabinoid receptor sites is anandamide. Anandamide is highly involved in the chemical regulation of things like mood, memory, appetite, and pain perception. Sometimes the body releases anandamide to help cope with the stress and pain of intense exercise (like runner's high). Cacao also contains anandamide inhibitors, two structural cousins of anandamide. What these chemicals do is inhibit the metabolism of anandamide, meaning they decrease the body's ability to process anandamide. This means that natural and/or plant-derived anandamide lingers in the body longer, drawing out the elated sensation.

"The Divine Lovers": Cacao and Vanilla. Cacao beans, nibs, powder, and butter with vanilla beans

Tryptophan (trip-tow-fan): Cacao contains significant quantities of the essential amino acid tryptophan. Obtaining tryptophan in the diet is necessary for the production of serotonin, a major neurotransmitter. Tryptophan reacts with vitamins B3 and B6 and, in the presence of magnesium, serotonin is produced. Since cacao contains all those nutrients (tryptophan, B3, B6, and magnesium), regular consumption of cacao ensures healthy serotonin levels. Serotonin is our "stress-defense shield" and typically lowers anxiety and increases our ability to fend off stress. Tryptophan also triggers production of other tryptomine neurotransmitters such as melatonin and dimethyl-tryptamine (DMT), both of which are associated with sleep. Large doses of cacao will usually produce such results, despite all the stimulating qualities cacao also possesses. Tryptophan is highly heat-volatile and is usually destroyed or severely damaged by cooking.

Raw, Organic, Fair-Trade Cacao

When choosing what kind of cacao beans/nibs/powder/butter to purchase, make sure the products are raw, organic, and fairly traded. Cacao comes in whole-bean form, shelled, and broken up "nib" form, and in the form of cacao powder that has had all the fat removed from it, but without additives and cooking. Cacao powder is the most versatile of the three forms, and the most accessible as it really delivers the full-on chocolate flavor. If purchasing whole beans, check for mold contamination as this can sometimes happen.

All three forms have their own various applications, and I recommend having all of them on hand if you are serious about cacao and raw desserts. Also available (which you must have!) is cacao butter, which is the same as "cocoa butter" only raw. Regular, even expensive cocoa butter is generally produced using very high heats and chemical solvents like hexane. Cacao butter is produced at a raw temperature and without chemicals. This stuff is amazing and has all sorts of uses, especially for making white-chocolate-themed desserts.

Cacao should ideally be stored in airtight, glass jars. Don't keep cacao in the fridge (except for cacao butter), as the moisture can trigger mold formation.

Again, please support fair-trade organic cacao growers, as more than 80% of the world's cacao crop comes from West Africa where horrible working conditions, including child slavery, degrade humanity on a daily basis (not to mention the pesticides). All the big candy companies get their chocolate from these West African growers, so please vote with your dollars for fair-trade, organic cacao!

Cacao is one of the main crops contributing to the preservation of the rainforest. Since cacao naturally thrives best underneath the canopy of larger trees in a jungle setting, organic cacao is a sustainably grown crop (which sells!). It is at the forefront of many plants that are helping to make the rainforest more valuable intact rather than destroyed. We can eat the most delicious, natural chocolate and save the rainforest at the same time! But only when the cacao is organic and fairly traded.

Making Truffles and Chocolate Cups

The majority of these recipes are meant to be paired with chocolate, either in truffle form or in the form of a chocolate cup. The recipes with "chocolate cup" in the title are designed to be used as such; however, they can also be made into truffles. Truffles and chocolate cups are both relatively easy things to construct and don't require a lot of specialized equipment, making these recipes easy and fun to create at home. You can make your own gourmet, raw, vegan chocolates at home using just a food processor and a blender!

TRUFFLE ASSEMBLY DIRECTIONS

1. **Scoop the Filling.** Once the filling has set to the point specified in the recipe, start scooping out little balls of the filling. The size of scoop can range from an actual truffle scoop to a small ice cream scoop, depending on how large you want the filling to be. We mainly use a small ice cream scoop that is 1½ inches wide, which is about the largest you would want the truffle to be. When deciding what size scoop to use, keep in mind that some fillings are stronger and more intense than others and will taste better when kept small. Place each scoop on some sort of non-stick surface that you can easily move in/out of the fridge. A teflex-lined sheet from a dehydrator works perfectly, but you can also use a non-stick baking sheet or wax paper.

2. **Chill the Scooped Fillings.** Place the scooped fillings in the fridge or freezer to firm them up before they get dipped in chocolate. Some fillings need to be firmer than others prior to dipping, and the recipe will specify this.

3. **Melt the Chocolate.** Melting raw chocolate requires constant attention so that it doesn't overheat. Melt the chocolate in a medium to large bowl sitting atop a pot of boiling water. The pot below will only need to have 1–2 inches of water in it, just enough to produce plenty of steam. If you have made your chocolate fresh, it is already melted and will probably only require a little bit of steaming, if any at all. If the chocolate has been made beforehand and is hard, you must first chop it up. Chop it up pretty small, as this will help it melt faster.

   The faster the chocolate melts, the less chance you have of overheating it. A lot of energy has gone into the production of the raw versions of cacao powder and butter, not to mention the extra money used to purchase them, so be attentive when melting raw chocolate so it does not overheat and lose some of its benefits. Do not take the chocolate above 115°. If you are using your finger as a gauge, don't take the chocolate a whole lot higher than body temperature. Having a thermometer is handy, and there are specific chocolate thermometers for this purpose.

   Stir the chocolate often while melting so that it maintains a consistent temperature. Once the chocolate is freely running off the spoon or spatula, it is ready to come off the steam and be used.

4. **Dip the Truffles.** Remove the chilled fillings from the fridge or freezer. Set them next to the bowl of melted chocolate. Have another non-stick surface sheet ready to set the dipped truffles on. Drop the undipped truffle into the bowl of chocolate and immediately lift it out using a fork. Gently tap the bottom of the fork against the edge of the bowl so the excess chocolate can drip off. Then lightly wipe the bottom of the fork against

the edge of the bowl to remove even more excess chocolate. Bring over to the prepared sheet and gently shimmy the truffle off the fork without touching it. You can also lightly nudge the truffle off the fork with your finger if necessary. Repeat this process until all the truffles are dipped. Depending on the recipe, a garnish may be called for, which is applied to the truffle immediately after dipping.

5. **Set the Truffles.** Move the sheet of dipped truffles back into the fridge or freezer to set the chocolate. Once chocolate has hardened, the truffles are ready to eat! Store uneaten truffles in the fridge in an airtight container.

CHOCOLATE CUP ASSEMBLY DIRECTIONS

1. **Get the Molds Ready.** If you have any special molds for making chocolate cups, obviously use those. Otherwise, an easy, cheap, and accessible mold alternative exists in the form of mini paper baking cups. These are similar to what you would use to make cupcakes, only they are smaller versions usually used for serving small cookies or baking mini-muffins. If you have mini-muffin pans that the paper cups fit perfectly into, use these for easier production. Line up the appropriate number of baking cups on a baking sheet that can be moved in/out of the fridge.

2. **Prepare the Filling.** Make the filling according to recipe directions. Once made, keep filling in a bowl out at room temperature, unless otherwise noted in recipe.

3. **Melt the Chocolate.** See Step 3 above in the truffle assembly directions.

4. **Pour and Set the Cup Bottoms.** Using a tablespoon, pour a small amount of chocolate onto the bottom of each cup (usually about ½ tablespoon). Now, using your finger, swirl the chocolate around the cup walls. You want to evenly coat the walls of your mold or paper cup. If you are using pre-made chocolate do not melt it down all the way. Thick chocolate

works better for this step since more chocolate will stick to the cup walls, making the final product less fragile. Transfer cups to the fridge or freezer until chocolate is set, only about 10–15 minutes. Return the cups to your working station.

5. **Pipe the Filling into the Cup.** Place part or all of the filling into a pastry bag. Proceed to pipe the filling into the prepared cups. Leave ¼ inch of room at the top that will be filled with chocolate. With your finger, lightly tap down the top of the filling to flatten it out. You can also use a spoon to fill the cups, but a pastry bag makes this step faster and easier.

6. **Finishing the Cups.** Fill the rest of the cup with chocolate. Using a tablespoon, drizzle enough chocolate into the cup to fill it all the way to the top (usually about ½ tablespoon). Garnish as suggested in recipe or with garnish of your choice.

7. **Set Cups in Fridge/Freezer.** Place cups in the fridge or freezer until they are set. They will be hard to the touch when done. Cups are now ready for serving or to be stored in an airtight container in the fridge. Enjoy!

USEFUL TIPS

Keep your double boiler going on low in case you need to briefly steam chocolate to thin it out. Having chocolate at the right consistency while you are dipping truffles is essential. Depending on room temperature and amount of chocolate you are working with, the chocolate may start to thicken/harden very quickly. A brief steam and stir is all that's needed.

With all chocolate work, keep absolutely everything that is coming in contact with the chocolate dry and clean. Water will unpleasantly mark your finished product or cause the melted chocolate to seize, meaning it will thicken and completely change consistency.

Raw Chocolate

Makes about 6 cups chocolate

3½ cups cacao butter

4 vanilla beans (scraped insides only)

1 cup + 3 tablespoons powdered sucanat (finely ground
   in coffee grinder)

⅓ cup agave syrup

¾ teaspoon salt

22 ounces cacao powder (weight)

Blend the melted cacao butter and scraped vanilla until vanilla is completely broken down and mixture is warm.

Pour 2 cups of blended vanilla-butter in your food processor (leave the remaining 1½ cups in the blender). Add to the processor half the amount of cacao powder and begin processing (1 minute).

Stop to add the salt and powdered sucanat. Resume processing (1 minute).

Resume blending the remaining 1½ cups vanilla-butter. While blender is running, slowly pour in the agave and blend until well combined. Add the blended agave portion to the food processor and resume processing (1 minute).

Stop to add the remaining cacao powder and process for an additional 2–3 minutes, scraping sides with spatula if needed.

Use chocolate as needed—pour into a bowl for dipping truffles or into molds for chocolates, or begin the tempering process if you are really ambitious! Tempering chocolate is a process of raising and lowering the temperatures to achieve the ideal crystalline structure of the chocolate. The temperatures are all in the raw range and go in this order: heat chocolate to 113°F (45°C), cool to 80°F (27°C), then reheat up to 88°F (31°C). Tempering is a time-consuming and very precise technique used to create chocolate that is stable at room temperature. Making chocolate does not require tempering, but untempered chocolate must be kept in the fridge.

Note: Sometimes chocolate will come out very thick. This may happen for several reasons, the most common one being that water has somehow gotten into the chocolate. Even just a very small amount of water may cause the chocolate to "seize" due to a chemical reaction. Seized chocolate actually contracts and becomes very thick. The best way to deal with this is to add more melted cacao butter, a tablespoon at a time, until the mixture thins out to the proper consistency. The ideal consistency is when chocolate can thickly coat a spoon and the excess can easily and smoothly run off it.

Make half a recipe if your processor has less than 6-cups capacity

Variations: Coconut and/or maple sugar can be substituted for the sucanat in this recipe. If you are substituting sweeteners, make sure it is in a dry form. We don't recommend substituting agave syrup or other liquid sweetener for the sucanat.

Storage and life span: Store chocolate in the fridge. Chocolate lasts for a long time. This chocolate will remain delicious for at least two months.

Raw Chocolate Sauce

Makes 2½ cups sauce

1 cup almond milk
2 ounces cacao powder (weight)
¼ cup cacao nibs
½ cup agave syrup
¼ cup liquid vanilla
4 ounces date paste (weight)
¼ teaspoon salt

Blend all ingredients until smooth and creamy. Pour into squeeze bottle or other container and use as needed.

Storage and life span: This chocolate sauce will keep for at least five days. Store in an airtight container in the fridge.

Raw Cacao Fudge

Makes 25 fudge squares

1 cup cacao butter
3 vanilla beans (scraped insides only)
1 cup agave syrup
½ cup cacao nibs (finely ground in coffee grinder)
8½ ounces cacao powder (weight)
¾ cup almond butter
½ teaspoon salt

Slice the vanilla beans in half lengthwise. With a spoon, thoroughly scrape the insides of the beans and add to blender. Add the melted cacao butter to the blender and blend until vanilla is totally broken down and mixture feels warm. Pour into a large mixing bowl; stir in the salt, agave, and almond butter by hand.

Grind the cacao beans/nibs in a coffee grinder until finely ground (be sure to wash and wipe the grinder free of coffee or whatever else was in there). Add to the bowl along with the cacao powder and stir by hand until smooth and there are no pockets of cacao powder.

Transfer mixture to a baking sheet or pan (8x8x2 inch is ideal), lined with heavy waxed paper. Use a spatula to get a smooth top. Set in the fridge or freezer until fudge becomes hard (20 minutes). Remove from fridge or freezer and pull fudge off the baking sheet onto a cutting board. Cut into the size and shapes you choose!

You must use waxed paper or teflex sheets, or the fudge will stick to the pan and the whole thing will become a big mess.

Variations: You can vary this fudge recipe by adding different elements like dried fruit or plant/flower essences. My favorite thing to add is dried raspberries. It's always best to dehydrate your own raspberries or other fruit if you have a dehydrator. That way you know it was dehydrated at a raw temperature (115° or below). Any dried berry tastes good in this fudge; also try goji berries, blueberries, or strawberries.

Substitutions of other nut butters for almond is another fun variation to play with. Try macadamia, hazelnut, pecan, cashew, or coconut butters. You can be creative with flavor additions as long as it is a small amount of a dry ingredient; otherwise the intensely explosive chocolate flavor of this fudge stands on its own.

Storage and life span: Fudge should ideally be stored in the fridge, although this fudge holds and lasts very well even out of fridge. Stays yummy for two to four weeks!

Super Cacao Balls

Makes 27 balls

2 cups cacao nibs
1 tablespoon maca powder
2 ounces cacao powder (weight)
1¼ teaspoon salt
¾ cup almond butter
⅓ cup yacon syrup
3 tablespoons coconut oil
1 tablespoon liquid vanilla

Finely grind the cacao nibs in a coffee grinder or dry blender. Mix all ingredients by hand in a bowl until mixture is consistent. Scoop out balls using a small ice cream scoop. Balls can be served immediately or placed in fridge to firm up first.

Variation: You can replace the maca powder with any other powdered superfood. For a delicious, spicy version simply add a half teaspoon cayenne or more to taste.

Storage and life span: These balls will keep for at least two weeks! Store in an airtight container in the fridge.

Mighty Chocolate Nut-Seed Bars

Makes 24 bars

3 cups almonds
¾ cup pumpkin seeds
1⅓ cups sunflower seeds
⅔ cup cacao nibs
¾ cup sesame seeds
1 cup + 2 tablespoons coconut flakes
⅔ cup goji berries
¾ cup hempseeds
½ cup flax seeds
1¼ teaspoons salt
1 vanilla bean (scraped insides only)
¾ cup agave syrup
¾ cup cacao butter
¾ cup almond butter

Raw Cacao Fudge, Mighty Chocolate Nut-Seed Bars, and Super Cacao Balls

Lightly process the almonds until about a quarter of them are still mostly whole.

Using a coffee grinder, finely powder the flax seeds and half the amount of sesame seeds.

Blend the scraped vanilla with melted cacao butter. Combine all dry ingredients in a bowl and toss until well mixed.

Add the blended cacao-vanilla butter, agave syrup, and almond butter and mix by hand until all ingredients are thoroughly combined.

Remove 3 cups of mixture and process until it is mostly broken down. It should resemble a moist pie crust. Add back to rest of mixture and thoroughly re-incorporate.

Using a teflex sheet or heavy waxed paper, line a baking pan (8x8x2 inch) and spread mixture evenly into the pan. Keep thickness as consistent as possible, firmly pack, then smooth over the top with a spatula. Place in fridge or freezer until mixture is solid and hard to the touch (about 30 minutes).

Remove from pan and set block on cutting board. Using a sharp serrated knife, cut the block into whatever size pieces you wish. Once bars are cut, set in fridge or freezer to chill for 20–30 minutes before dipping in chocolate.

Take a baking sheet and top it with a teflex sheet or heavy waxed paper. Once bars are chilled and chocolate is ready, dip a half-inch of the bar in the melted chocolate (recipe on page 160). Place the dipped bars on the baking sheet and set in fridge or freezer until chocolate is hard. Of course, the dipping in chocolate step can be omitted and these bars will still be delicious by themselves.

Variations: Multiple ingredients lend themselves to variation in this recipe. You can substitute any other dry nut (such as hazelnuts or pistachios) for the almonds. The goji berries can be replaced with any other dried berry or fruit (such as mulberries, cranberries, or apples). For a really low-glycemic version, substitute yacon syrup for the agave syrup and add some spices like cinnamon and ginger.

Storage and life span: Store these bars in the fridge. They will keep for many weeks.

Brazil Nut Ganache Truffles

Makes 22 large truffles

BRAZIL NUT CREAM
1¼ cups Brazil nuts
1¼ cups water

Blend nuts and water together until nuts are completely broken down. Allow to steep for 10 minutes, then strain the Brazil nut cream.

GANACHE
Brazil Nut Cream (see above)
6½ tablespoons agave syrup
3 ounces cacao powder (weight)
¼ teaspoon salt
3 vanilla beans (scraped insides only)
½ cup cacao butter

Blend the Brazil nut cream with the agave, cacao powder, and salt until smooth and creamy. Set aside. Blend the melted cacao butter with the scraped vanilla beans. Once vanilla is thoroughly blended and oil is warm, slowly pour in (while blender is running) the Brazil nut cream–cacao mixture and continue blending until well incorporated. Pour into a container and set in fridge overnight, or until mixture has firmed up enough to easily scoop.

Scoop out truffles using a 1½-inch ice cream scoop and set on a non-stick baking sheet (or dehydrator tray with teflex sheet). Freeze the scooped ganache before dipping in melted chocolate (recipe, page 160). Process some Brazil nuts and either roll entire truffle in processed Brazil nuts (you will need about 2 cups of nuts for this) or garnish each truffle with a light sprinkling of processed Brazil nut. Whichever way you decide to garnish them, it must be done immediately after dipping, as the frozen truffle will make the chocolate harden right away. If you choose to roll truffle in Brazil nuts (preferred method), finish by striping a light amount of chocolate over the top of the truffle. Truffles are now done, although they may still be slightly frozen in the middle. You may want to put them all in the fridge for several hours before serving.

Storage and life span: These truffles will keep for at least four days. Store in an airtight container in the fridge.

Brazil Nut Ganache and Macadamia Butter Truffles

Macadamia Butter Truffles

Makes about 18 large truffles

1½ cups macadamia-cashew butter
2 cups macadamias
½ vanilla bean (scraped insides only)
3 tablespoons agave syrup
½ teaspoon salt

Lightly process the macadamias so that they are slightly broken down but mostly chunky. Transfer to a bowl and toss with salt. Add the scraped vanilla bean to bowl and incorporate by rubbing it between your hands with the processed nuts. Remove and discard any larger fibrous vanilla bits that may be in there.

Add the macadamia-cashew butter and agave syrup and stir until all ingredients are well combined. Put entire bowl in freezer, stirring occasionally until mixture has considerably hardened up (about 30 minutes). Scoop out truffles using a small ice cream scoop and lay on a non-stick surface. Place scooped truffles in freezer until hard. Dip truffles in melted chocolate (recipe on page 160). See truffle assembly directions, page 156.

Optional: Immediately after dipping, sprinkle some processed macadamias on top or place a whole nut on top for decoration. You can also finish this truffle by striping a light amount of chocolate over the top.

Storage and life span: These truffles will keep for at least one week. Store in an airtight container in the fridge.

Almond Butter Cups

Makes 18 fillings

1 cup almond butter
¼ cup cacao butter
¼ cup agave syrup
2 tablespoons powdered sucanat (finely ground in
    coffee grinder)
¾ teaspoon salt

Mix all ingredients by hand in a bowl. Place mixture in fridge or freezer.

Follow chocolate cup assembly directions, page 158. Garnish top of cup with several almonds.

Storage and life span: This filling will keep for at least one week. Store chocolate items made with this filling in an airtight container in the fridge.

Hazelnut Amaretto Cups
Makes 14 fillings

1 cup hazelnuts
½ cup agave syrup
1 tablespoon liquid vanilla
¼ cup cacao butter
2 teaspoons almond extract
¾ teaspoon salt

Process hazelnuts and salt until nuts are as broken down as possible. Stop to scrape sides of processor bowl as needed.

Add the agave, liquid vanilla, and almond extract and process until smooth. Now add the melted cacao butter and continue processing until smooth. Transfer mixture to a bowl and place in fridge or freezer to chill. When the consistency has slightly thickened and is not too sticky (about 10 minutes), proceed with chocolate cup assembly directions, page 158. Garnish top of cup with several whole hazelnuts.

Variation: Try using hazelnut extract in place of or combined with the almond extract.

Storage and life span: This filling will keep for at least one week. Store chocolate items made with this filling in an airtight container in the fridge.

Almond-Coconut Joy Truffles

Makes 30 truffles

1¼ cups powdered coconut flakes (process in coffee grinder
  or blender with dry blade)
2¼ cups coconut flakes (medium-sized flakes)
½ vanilla bean (scraped insides only)
⅔ cup agave syrup
7 tablespoons coconut butter (see Chapter 1, page 7)
½ cup almonds
¼ teaspoon salt

Place powdered coconut and coconut flakes in bowl and mix in
scraped vanilla bean. Rub portions of mixture between your hands
to really break up the vanilla chunks and evenly distribute. Once
mixture is thoroughly speckled with vanilla bean, remove any larger
fibrous chunks of the vanilla and discard.

Melt down the coconut butter over a double boiler, stirring as
it melts. Add the melted coconut butter and agave to mixture and
stir by hand until thoroughly combined.

Place entire bowl in fridge. You want the mixture to slightly
harden before scooping. Stir several times while in fridge so it is
consistently hardened. There is a point where it is perfect to scoop
into balls, probably after only 20 minutes. You don't want it to
harden nearly all the way or it is very difficult to scoop properly.

Using a small ice cream scoop, begin forming the truffles in the
following order: scoop a little mixture, press in one almond, scoop a
little more mixture, press in another single almond, and close up the
bottom with more mixture, scraping it smooth to create a flat bottom. There should be two almonds in each truffle, which is roughly
a half-cup of almonds total (of course you can add more almonds to
each truffle or omit them entirely).

Chill the formed truffles in the fridge or freezer until fairly solid
to the touch (about 25 minutes). Using a fork, dip truffles in melted

chocolate (recipe on page 160). See truffle assembly directions, page 156.

Variations: Try using a different nut, like macadamias, Brazil nuts, or pistachios. Or make it a nut-free coconut truffle. Regular virgin coconut oil can be substituted for the coconut butter, but the results won't be the same.

Note: To get the proper texture, medium-grade coconut flakes must be used. Don't use finely dessicated coconut flakes. The coconut butter used here is the kind mentioned in Chapter 1. It is an amazingly delicious and decadent actual butter, like almond or peanut butter. This coconut butter created a real distinction between coconut "oil" and "butter" (usually hardened coconut oil is referred to as "butter"). The meat of the mature coconut is creamed (at low heat) to create this incredible product. This ingredient is really what makes this truffle so outstanding, and we don't recommend making this candy unless you have this specific item.

Storage and life span: Store in fridge. These should remain fresh for at least two weeks.

Maca Malt Cups

Makes about 17 fillings

¾ cup Brazil nuts (4 ounces weight)
⅓ cup agave syrup
1 tablespoon liquid vanilla
¼ cup maca
¼ teaspoon salt
¼ cup cacao butter

Process Brazil nuts with salt until they are completely broken down. Then add in the agave and liquid vanilla. Continue processing until smooth. Transfer mixture to a bowl and incorporate by hand the

Maca Malt Cup and Almond-Coconut Joy Truffle

melted cacao butter and maca. Stir until well combined and there are no chunks of maca. Set aside in a bowl at room temperature.

Follow chocolate cup assembly directions, page 158. To garnish, slowly slice a Brazil nut in half (lengthwise) using a serrated paring knife. Gently lay and push halved Brazil nuts (flat side facing up) in middle of cup.

Storage and life span: This filling will keep at least one week. Store chocolate items made with this filling in an airtight container in the fridge.

Açaí Cups

Makes 14 fillings

⅓ cup açaí powder (2 ounces weight)
½ cup agave syrup
⅛ teaspoon salt
¾ cup coconut flakes
2 tablespoons cacao butter

Powder the coconut flakes as fine as possible in a coffee grinder or dry blender. Process all ingredients until just combined; over-processing will cause the oil to separate. Set aside in a bowl at room temperature. Follow chocolate cup assembly directions, page 158.

Storage and life span: This filling will keep at least one week. Store chocolate items made with this filling in an airtight container in the fridge.

Vanilla-Hempseed Cups

Makes 22 fillings

2 cups hempseeds
6 tablespoons agave syrup
¼ teaspoon salt
3 vanilla beans (scraped insides only)
¼ cup cacao butter

Blend the scraped vanilla with the melted cacao butter and agave syrup on low speed until vanilla is totally broken down. Transfer mixture to a bowl. Add the remaining half-cup of hempseeds to bowl and mix by hand until well combined. Set aside in a bowl at room temperature.

Follow chocolate cup assembly directions, page 158. Garnish top of cup with a generous sprinkling of hempseeds.

Storage and life span: This filling will keep for at least one week. Store chocolate items made with this filling in an airtight container in the fridge.

Peppermint Cups

Makes 15 fillings

⅔ cup soaked cashews
½ cup coconut flakes
⅓ cup agave syrup
⅓ bunch spearmint (leaves only)—about ½ cup
¼ teaspoon salt
1½ teaspoons lemon juice
¼ cup coconut oil (unscented)
1 tablespoon peppermint extract

Blend the agave syrup, mint leaves, lemon, and cashews until smooth (you will need a plunger for this). Powder the coconut flakes as fine as possible in a coffee grinder or dry blender. Transfer to food processor with rest of ingredients and process until as smooth as possible. Place entire bowl in fridge or freezer to thicken. Stir several times while mixture is firming up for a consistent texture. Allow to chill 20–30 minutes or until mixture is firm enough to be used with a pastry bag. Follow chocolate cup assembly directions, page 158.

SPECIAL GREEN SWIRL GARNISH

Blend ½ cup melted cacao butter with 1 teaspoon powdered green food and 5 large spearmint leaves. Spoon about ¼ teaspoon on top of each cup (before cup is set). This mixture will need to be stirred

White Chocolate Lavender Cups and Peppermint Cups and Medallions

often while working with it. With a chopstick, lightly swirl the green butter into the chocolate.

Variation: You can also create peppermint "medallions" with this filling. Scoop a small amount of chilled filling and gently flatten by hand into a disc shape (about the size of a quarter). Chill the medallions and dip in chocolate.

Note: Do not over-blend or over-process the filling as this will darken the color.

Storage and life span: This filling will keep for at least four days. Store chocolate items made with this filling in an airtight container in the fridge.

White Chocolate Lavender Cups

Makes 18 fillings

½ cup agave syrup

2½ teaspoons dry lavender flowers (powder first in coffee grinder)

1 vanilla bean (scraped insides only)

⅔ cup soaked cashews

⅔ cup powdered coconut flakes (use a coffee grinder)

⅓ cup cacao butter

½ teaspoon salt

Blend agave syrup, lavender, and vanilla until warm and lavender is totally broken down. Add melted cacao butter and continue blending. Add cashews and blend until smooth (use plunger). Transfer to food processor, add coconut and salt, and process until smooth. Place entire bowl in fridge or freezer to thicken. Stir several times while mixture is firming up for a consistent texture. Allow to chill 10–20 minutes or until mixture is firm enough to be used with a pastry bag.

Follow chocolate cup assembly directions, page 158. Garnish with a very light sprinkling of lavender flowers.

Storage and life span: This filling will keep for at least four days. Store chocolate items made with this filling in an airtight container in the fridge.

CHAPTER 8

Irish Moss

Trust

Trusting is one of the most powerful choices we can make. To trust is a choice that we make without evidence, without reasons, and without expectations of the result. It is an individual choice that we make on a daily basis, constantly recommitting ourselves to trusting the perfection of everything, our intuition, and the process of life itself. Trusting that each one of our experiences is perfect and realizing how they contribute to the creation of ourselves brings us to a place of acceptance and peace of mind. When we are not choosing to trust, we allow doubt and fear to shape our view of the world and ourselves. When we experience this doubt and fear it is the perfect moment to remind ourselves to trust, and also to remember that no logical understanding is necessary to do so. The process starts within us and will be reflected in the world around us.

The perfect opportunity to practice trust is when we are faced with the unknown. Many of the ingredients in our recipes are not commonly used or even heard of. Raw desserts in general are little known, and they are often doubted simply because they are different. Trust that you are capable of learning the art of raw desserts and do not fear using a new ingredient. An ingredient such as Irish moss might be intimidating if we are not familiar with it. Indeed it is unique, especially when used in desserts. Trust the Irish moss! You will be amazed at the results this ingredient brings.

Irish moss is truly a miracle food. Its wide range of health benefits makes this amazing plant one of the world's top superfoods. This beautiful seaweed really catapulted our raw creations into a new world of desserts. The textures this one ingredient can create are unparalleled in the raw world. Irish moss is the ideal addition for desserts with a light, fluffy, and soft texture.

This seaweed does not require heat activation, making it perfect for raw cuisine. It can completely gelatinize something, turning any type of liquid into "jello" simply by blending. This quality makes it a wonderful raw and vegan alternative to gelatin. Irish moss has a plethora of uses in both sweet and savory foods. We use it extensively in our desserts; and in savory raw cuisine Irish moss is great in things like dressings, sauces, juices, patés, and quiches. Our desserts with Irish moss are definitely the healthiest, and certainly the most unique!

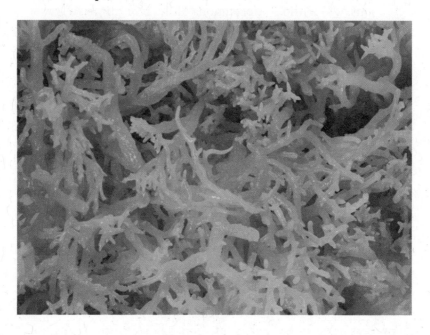

Recipes

Equipment Needed

- Blender
- Measuring cups
- Measuring spoons
- Spatulas
- Bowls
- Scale
- Small cups or flan molds
  (only for Crème Caramel)

About Irish Moss

Irish moss *(Chrondrus crispus)* is a type of seaweed that is purple to green when fresh; when cured and dried it turns to a yellow-brown transparent color. Other common names for Irish moss are pearl moss, carrageen, red seaweed, or chondrus. This algae appears at low tide on all the shores of the Atlantic and comes from a genus of about fifteen species of marine algae. These plants, ranging in size from 3–12 inches, are collected wild, growing on rocks and stones in pools and shallow saltwater, and may be harvested by boat using a rake and by hand from the submerged rocks. It is found along the shorelines of Canada, New England, Europe, and the Caribbean.

Like all sea vegetables, Irish moss is rich in minerals and has astonishing detoxifying properties. One of its common names, carrageen, is derived from a village in southeastern Ireland (Carragheen) where the seaweed is plentiful. During the potato famine of the mid-nineteenth century, thousands of beleaguered Irish saved themselves from starvation by eating the humble, bushy seaweed known as Irish moss. Irish immigrants who found it growing in Canada and on the New England shores were the first to harvest and use it in America, and this is how the plant became known as "Irish moss."

The entire plant, which is dried and then soaked to swell back to its original size, is used medicinally and for culinary purposes. Used commercially, it is included in cosmetics as a skin softener in creams and lotions and as a rinse for dry hair. Irish moss is a stabilizing agent for the food industry in dairy products, desserts, salad dressings, and sauces. It is used in the pharmaceutical industry to stabilize cod liver oil and toothpaste, and has a wide variety of other commercial uses in the textile, leather, brewing, printing (as an ink), and paint industries. Irish moss has a high mucilage content, sulphur compounds, protein, iodine, bromine, beta-carotene, calcium, iron, magnesium, manganese, phosphorus, potassium, selenium, zinc, gel-forming polysaccharides (known as carragheenans), pectin, B vitamins, and vitamin C.

Health Benefits of Irish Moss

Respiratory System

Irish moss has a soothing effect on virtually all the mucous membranes throughout the body. This sweet, salty, mucilaginous herb has a softening effect on tissues and helps many respiratory problems including bronchitis and pneumonia. It is especially effective for pulmonary (lung) conditions, with its ability to absorb liquid and eliminate it from the body. As an expectorant, Irish moss relieves dry coughs, and the high mucilage content alleviates catarrh (inflammation) of the nasal passages and eases sore throat.

Digestion and Thyroid Function

Irish moss soothes the mucous membranes of the digestive tract, and the high mucilage content helps to ease gastritis, dyspepsia, nausea, heartburn, and indigestion and is also used to prevent vomiting. Irish moss is a mild and effective laxative and soothes inflamed tissues of the intestinal tract, providing help for intestinal disorders. In addition, Irish moss is said to absorb toxins from the bowel and draw radiation poison from the body. Irish moss is rich in iodine, supplying the nutrient throughout the intestinal tract. Iodine is highly important in supporting good thyroid gland health and relieving the many problems associated with poor thyroid function and iodine deficiency (goiter, fatigue, inability to tolerate cold, slow heart rate, low metabolism, poor skin and hair condition, etc.).

Weight Loss

Irish moss helps to reduce the appetite by virtue of its ability to absorb moisture, increasing the feeling of "fullness." The raised metabolic rate caused by improved thyroid function (resulting from Irish moss's iodine content) helps to increase energy, burn fat, and may be helpful in weight-loss regimens.

Blood Pressure

Because Irish moss contains blood-thinning properties and is considered an anticoagulant, early research has claimed that Irish moss can reduce high blood pressure and the risk of arteriosclerosis.

Skin Care

Irish moss is wonderful used externally. It softens and soothes the skin and other exposed tissue. It eases sunburn, chapped skin, dermatitis, eczema, psoriasis, and rashes. It counters premature aging when used topically for smoothing wrinkles.

Pregnancy

Irish moss is great for pregnant women. It is highly beneficial in supporting the healthy production of amniotic fluid. After birth, the baby benefits from the nourishment it adds to breast milk.

Basic Directions for Using Irish Moss

Soaking Irish Moss

Properly soaking the Irish moss has a huge impact on the entire recipe. Closely following these directions will result in an ingredient that is as consistent as possible for the best results in the finished product. Irish moss soaked according to these directions and stored covered with water will last for at least a week when kept in the fridge in an airtight container. After one week you may see a difference in color and size. The Irish moss may look transparent and swollen. If this is the case you will need to add an additional ¼–½ ounce of Irish moss to each recipe. Soak only the amount you think you will use for one week.

Irish moss before soaking, properly soaked, and overly soaked

Unsoaked Irish moss will last in an airtight container in the fridge for months.

All preparation steps for Irish moss use cold water only. Rinsing or soaking in warm or hot water will cause the Irish moss to lose its mucilaginous gelling properties, making it less effective in these recipes.

Directions for Rinsing/Soaking Irish Moss

* Thoroughly rinse small amounts of the Irish moss under cold running water. Ideally use filtered water. This process should remove any presence of sand, other seaweeds, or any small little plastic treads (usually light blue or red in color) which are left over from harvesting.
* As you wash the Irish moss one piece at a time, place the rinsed pieces in an empty container. Whatever size container you are using, do not fill it up more than three-quarters of the way.
* Once finished with rinsing, fill the container with water. With your hand mix the Irish moss inside the container (if container is too small, shake well with lid on). This will create friction and release more impurities. Drain the water and repeat two more times. The water from the last rinse should be really clean. If not, repeat one more time.
* Now fill the container with water again, completely covering the Irish moss. Put lid on container and place in fridge for at least 24 hours before using.
* Don't rinse the Irish moss after the soaking process is complete, and don't drain or replace the soaking water.

Using Irish Moss in the Recipes

Irish moss needs to be blended extremely well. All recipes using Irish moss specify the amount of liquid (usually 1 cup total) along with the measurement (in weight) of Irish moss. These ingredients are blended first until the Irish moss is completely broken down and smooth. This is what we call the "initial blending phase." Then the remaining ingredients can be added and the recipe completed.

Irish Moss Blending Directions

* Using a scale, weigh the amount of Irish moss called for in the recipe. When measuring Irish moss always double-check the weight. Remove from scale, dry any excess water from the scale top, and weigh the Irish moss again. The first measurement may contain up to a quarter (¼) ounce of water, and this will affect the recipe.
* Coarsely chop the Irish moss and add to blender.
* Add to blender the specified amount of liquid required for the initial blending phase.
* Blend until mixture becomes smooth and jelly-like, and there are no visible small pieces of Irish moss. The amount of time this requires will vary greatly, depending on what kind of blender you are using and/or how sharp the blade is.
* There will always be small pieces of unblended Irish moss on the sides of the blender and underneath the lid. Stop blending and with a spatula scrape down the sides of the blender, as well as underneath the lid. Resume blending until all the Irish moss is completely broken down.
* Stop blending and add the remaining ingredients of the recipe you are making, unless the recipe calls for coconut oil and lecithin, which always go in last.

USEFUL TIPS

Whole-food Irish moss is available but usually hard to find unless you are looking on the Internet. (Café Gratitude is the only place we know of that sells bags of whole Irish moss.) It should come covered in sand and salt and have a strong oceanic smell. This is perfectly normal. If properly prepared, the flavor and odor of the Irish moss become totally unnoticeable with all the other flavors it is being combined with.

More widely available is the flaked and dehydrated Irish moss. This form of Irish Moss has the same gelling abilities as the whole-food Irish moss, but we strongly do *not* recommend using it. It has an overwhelming seaweed flavor that you can't wash off. Going through the trouble of obtaining this ingredient fresh is well worth it. It keeps in the fridge very well, which means you can safely stock up and have it on hand.

For an easy way to use Irish moss medicinally, try gelatinizing some water. Simply blend 1 ounce Irish moss with 1½ cups water. Blend until Irish moss is completely broken down. You can keep this in a container in the fridge for at least two weeks. Add 2–3 table-spoons (or more) to juices or smoothies and blend it up briefly before drinking. This is a great way to benefit from the healing powers of Irish moss without making some elaborate raw creation.

Recipes that call for Irish moss always set better in the fridge than the freezer.

Coconut Meringue

Makes 2½ cups meringue

¾ ounce Irish moss (weight)
¼ cup water
⅔ cup coconut milk

Blend until Irish moss is completely broken down (see Irish moss blending directions, page 184). Add to blender:

1 cup coconut milk
¼ cup coconut meat (wet measure)
½ cup soaked cashews (wet measure)
5 tablespoons agave syrup
½ tablespoon vanilla
1 teaspoon lemon juice
⅛ teaspoon salt

Blend well until smooth and creamy, then add:

1 tablespoon lecithin
½ cup + 1 tablespoon coconut oil

Resume blending until lecithin and oil are fully incorporated. Pour into container and set in fridge until slightly firm, with a soft consistency. For the best texture, ideally set in fridge overnight.

Storage and life span: Store in an airtight container in the fridge. Meringue will be good for at least three days.

Fresh Fruit Parfait

Makes 6 servings

One full recipe of Coconut Meringue (page 185)
2 packs of fresh berries, about 12 ounces total

To assemble parfaits, place a spoonful of meringue at the bottom of each parfait glass (or any 8-ounce clear glass). Layer 1 heaping tablespoon of berries on top of the meringue. If using strawberries, chop the fruit in small pieces. Alternate meringue and berries until the glass is almost full (about four layers of meringue and three layers of fruit). Always finish with a layer of meringue on the top. Decorate the top layer with a single berry and fresh mint. Parfait is now ready to be served.

Variations: You can use any kind of fruit for this dessert. The best combination is a berry medley such as strawberry/blueberry/blackberry/raspberry.

Storage and life span: Store in the fridge for up to two days.

Strawberry Parfait

Makes 6 servings

1 ounce Irish moss (weight)
1 cup almond milk

Blend ingredients until Irish moss is completely broken down (see Irish moss blending directions, page 184). Add to blender:

3 cups chopped strawberries (12 ounces weight)
½ cup agave syrup
2 tablespoons liquid vanilla
2 tablespoons lemon juice
⅛ teaspoon salt

Blend well until smooth and creamy, then add:

2 tablespoons lecithin
½ cup coconut oil

Resume blending until lecithin and oil are fully incorporated. Pour into parfait glasses or other serving glass. Set in fridge for 30–45 minutes. Garnish with fresh strawberries.

Variations: You can use other types of fresh berries such as blueberries, raspberries, and blackberries. This recipe is incredible combined with the Coconut Meringue (page 185) and the Magnificent Chocolate Mousse (page 188) to create a Neapolitan parfait. Simply layer the three recipes, alternating flavors, in parfait glasses.

Storage and life span: This parfait is best on the day it is made but will keep for at least two days. Store covered parfaits in the fridge.

Coconut Meringue and Fresh Fruit Parfait, Magnificent Chocolate Mousse, and Neapolitan Parfait

Magnificent Chocolate Mousse

Makes 6 servings

3/4 ounce Irish moss (weight)
¼ cup water
¾ cup almond milk

Blend until Irish moss is completely broken down (see Irish moss blending directions, page 184). Add to the blender:

1½ cups almond milk
¼ cup date paste (wet measure)
½ cup agave syrup
1½ ounces cacao powder (weight)
3 tablespoons liquid vanilla
⅛ teaspoon salt

Blend well until smooth and creamy, then add:

1½ tablespoons lecithin
6 tablespoons coconut oil

Resume blending until lecithin and oil are fully incorporated. Pour mousse into parfait glasses or other serving glass. Set in fridge for 30–45 minutes. Garnish with cacao nibs, whole almonds, or loose berries.

Variations: You can replace the almond milk with any other kind of nut milk.

Storage and life span: Mousse is best on the day it is made, but it will keep for at least three days. Store covered mousse cups in the fridge.

Irish Moss Glaze

Makes about 1 cup

½ ounce Irish moss (weight)
¾ cup apple juice
2 tablespoons orange juice
1 tablespoon liquid vanilla
1 tablespoon agave syrup
Small pinch salt

Blend all ingredients until Irish moss is completely broken down (see Irish moss blending directions, page 184).

Variations: This recipe is specifically for our raw Fruit Tarts (pages 40–43) but can also be used to make a deliciously healthy fruit salad. Toss about 4 cups of fresh fruit (any kind) with this glaze and serve.

Storage and life span: Keep this glaze in an airtight container in the fridge. Glaze will last for at least four days.

Crème Caramel

Makes 6 servings

1 ounce Irish moss (weight)
1½ cups coconut milk

Blend Irish moss with the coconut milk until smooth and creamy (see Irish moss blending directions, page 184). Add to blender:

¾ cup agave syrup
6 tablespoons liquid vanilla
¾ cup macadamias (4 ounces weight)
⅛ teaspoon salt
¹⁄₁₆ teaspoon turmeric
½ teaspoon yacon syrup

Resume blending until macadamias have completely broken down and mixture is consistent. Pour even amounts into 6 small cups (cups should hold 6–8 ounces) or crème caramel/flan molds. Set in fridge or freezer until firm to the touch (20–30 minutes).

Remove from fridge or freezer and run a knife or small spatula around the inside edge of the cup/mold to easily release the Crème Caramel.

When serving Crème Caramel you will need:

6 tablespoons yacon syrup

Crème Caramel

Drizzle on the center of each plate a half tablespoon of yacon syrup. Now flip the cup/mold upside-down onto the plate on top of the yacon syrup. Finish each serving by drizzling another half tablespoon yacon syrup on top of the Crème Caramel. Serve immediately.

Storage and life span: Store in the cup/mold in the fridge for up to a week. Use the yacon syrup when ready to serve.

Ingredient Information

Oneness

Oneness—such a big word with a very simple meaning: everything is connected. If we can understand how everything we do "does" affect others, we can understand the concept of oneness. It's not difficult to comprehend when we can see the immediate results of our actions. To fully understand oneness we need to realize how all our actions, thoughts, and beliefs *do* affect everything around us in ways we may never know or be aware of.

As part of the "one" we have the power to change the whole. To be part of the whole means to share equal responsibility in the creation of those changes. We know when we feel whole. We feel generous, compassionate, fulfilled, and loved. Separation is an illusion we all fall prey to. We struggle when we don't feel the "oneness" of our existence. Every time we create separation between ourselves and others or between ourselves and the Earth, we experience loneliness and sadness. We tend to constantly divide and separate everything, classifying and categorizing all things. Separation always creates some kind of conflict. Judgment is one of the expressions of separation. When we judge others for something we dislike or don't agree with, we automatically separate ourselves from it. At these times there is always an opportunity to see ourselves in a new way, reflected in somebody else.

We can all actually make a big difference in someone's life just by sharing a smile walking down the street. We may shift that person's experience, and that person will also affect other people. We may never know the ripple effect of that smile. Sometimes it takes very little to create the most profound transformation.

Every ingredient in every recipe is equally important. The ingredients we use are extremely varied and come from all over the world. These ingredients and recipes have their roots in many different traditions and cultures. They are a physical, edible expression of oneness!

The following pages provide information about most of the ingredients used in this book.

Açaí

Açaí *(Euterpe oleracea)* is a vibrant purple fruit from the Amazon palmberry, considered to be one of the most nutritious fruits in the world. Açaí (pronounced ah-sigh-ee) is full of amino acids, antioxidants, fiber, trace minerals, and essential fatty acids. It contains ten to thirty times more antioxidants than red wine. Açaí is thought to promote superior cardiovascular and gastrointestinal health, and to increase energy, strength, and mental acuity. It is also beneficial in balancing cholesterol levels.

Agave Nectar (Syrup)

The agave plant has long been cultivated in the hilly, semi-arid areas of Mexico. The species that produces agave syrup is the blue agave *(Agave tequilana).* From ancient days Central Americans have considered the plant sacred. They believed the liquid from this plant purified the body and soul. The conquering Spaniards took these juices and fermented them, leading to the creation of tequila. The juice or nectar is located in the pineapple-shaped heart of the plant. The agave plant has long been harvested for a variety of uses, including food, drink, and clothing.

Agave is about 90% fructose and 10% glucose. Natural fructose has a very low glycemic value so it won't overstimulate the production of insulin, making agave a much safer sugar alternative for some diabetics and people with sugar sensitivities.

Agave, unlike fructose sweeteners that are produced chemically, contains no sulfur dioxide, hydrochloric acid, or other harmful toxins. Agave nectar comes in light, amber, and dark varieties. We recommend the light or amber kinds in most desserts because the dark agave has a stronger, different flavor and has sometimes been heated.

Almonds

Almonds are very nutritious and are generally believed to be the most alkaline of all the nuts. They are high in magnesium, potassium, vitamins E and B2, dietary fiber, and the essential amino acid tryptophan. They are also high in monounsaturated fat, which helps reduce the risk of heart disease. Almonds are a great source of manganese and copper, two trace minerals essential for the production of the key enzyme superoxide dismutase. This enzyme disarms free radicals produced within our mitochondria (which is known as the "energy production factory" in our cells), thus helping to keep our energy level high.

Almonds are classified into two categories: Sweet *(Prunus amygdalus dulcis)* and Bitter *(Prunus amygdalus amara)*. Sweet almonds are the type we eat; and bitter almonds are used to make almond oil and flavoring agents for food and liqueurs such as amaretto. Bitter almonds are mostly inedible by themselves, as they contain several toxic substances (these toxins are removed in the processing of the oil). Almonds are notorious for being a crop that needs a lot of love and attention, thus making them one of the most pesticide-sprayed crops. This is the reason why organic almonds are so expensive. Support organic, raw almonds!

Apples

Everybody knows the apple. It is probably the most common and popular fruit there is. Harvested in the fall, apples are the fruit of a small deciduous tree *(Malus domestica/sieversii)*. Apples have a pretty amazing history; they are likely the earliest cultivated tree. There are more than 7,500 known varieties with different cultivars for temperate and sub-tropical climates, although most people have been exposed to only the most popular kinds like Red Delicious and Granny Smith. Apples can be sweet, tart, soft and smooth, or crisp and crunchy.

Always eat and use apples with their skins, since that is where most of the nutrients and flavor are. Apples are a fantastic source of both soluble and insoluble fiber. Soluble fiber such as pectin actually helps to prevent cholesterol buildup in the lining of blood vessel walls, thus reducing the risk of heart disease and other cholesterol-related diseases. Insoluble fiber provides bulk in the intestinal tract, holding water to cleanse and move food through more quickly and efficiently. Apples are high in vitamin C, phosphorus, potassium, calcium, and the trace mineral boron. They also contain valuable phytonutrients, especially quercetin, which has powerful antioxidant, anti-histimine, and anti-inflammatory effects. Quercetin has also been proven to inhibit the reproduction of cancer cells.

Bananas

Bananas *(Musa sapienta)* are the fruit of a giant herbaceous plant belonging to the same family as the lily and the orchid. Believed to have originated in Malaysia, the banana tree is thought to be close to a million years old. The bananas develop on a large flower spike after its cluster of purple flowers have blossomed. They grow in tropical and subtropical climates, with the main world producers being India, Brazil, Ecuador, and Indonesia.

For hundreds of years the difficulty of transporting this fragile fruit rendered it unavailable to most people. Now bananas are everywhere, usually stored in giant warehouses under closely controlled temperatures, often exposed to ethylene gas in order to artificially accelerate the ripening process.

There are three distinct species: sweet bananas, plantains or cooking bananas, and the inedible variety. There are many different kinds of sweet bananas, ranging in size and qualities of starchy or sweet. They are usually harvested while still green, as they are more flavorful when allowed to ripen off the plant. Bananas are an excellent source of potassium and vitamin B6 and are also rich in riboflavin, folic acid, and magnesium.

Blackberries

Blackberries *(Rubus fruticosus)* belong to the same family as the strawberry and raspberry. They grow in fields, woods, and gardens and can climb over walls and any other obstacles on their path. Blackberries are native to temperate climates and grow in Europe, North America, Australia, and the British Isles. The plant itself is usually a thorny shrub that produces beautiful clusters of delicate pink or white flowers. Blackberries are a composite of small juicy fruits called "drupelets," and each fruit contains a seed.

There are many different colors of blackberry. The most common are black, burgundy, red, and yellowish-white. There are more than a thousand varieties of blackberry known and grown all over the world. Blackberries are a good source of vitamin C, potassium, magnesium, and copper. They have astringent, cleansing, and laxative properties.

Blackberries tend to spoil rapidly. The best way to enjoy them is fresh from the bush. Harvesting black-colored blackberries may be challenging since the fruit turns black before it is ripe. When they are perfectly ripe, the sweetest and least acidic, the fruit is softer and will come off easily from the stem. The morning is always the best time to harvest them.

Blueberries

The dearly loved and revered blueberry is the fruit of a shrub that belongs to the botanical Heath family, which includes cranberries, azalea, and mountain laurel. They are classified in the genus Vaccinium and are native to North America, where they grow throughout the forested and mountainous regions. There are many types of plants within this genus that produce blue berries that are often confused with real blueberries (such as the European bilberry). The most common cultivated variety is *Vaccinium corymbosum.*

Blueberries grow in clusters and range in size from that of a small pea to a marble. The skin color is deep, ranging from blue to maroon to purple-black. Inside is the sweet semi-transparent whitish flesh that encases many miniature seeds. Blueberries are nutrient-rich and extremely high in antioxidants. Anthocyanadins are the antioxidant compounds that give certain fruits and vegetables their blue, purple, and red colors. These potent phytonutrients are very good at neutralizing free radicals.

"Phytonutrients" is the general term for health-promoting chemical compounds that come from edible plants. Regarding human physiology, "free radicals" are basically cells that have run amok. They have an imbalanced electron charge, which causes them to bounce about sporadically, crashing into things and resulting in serious cellular damage. Too many free radicals can result in various types of illness, including cancer. Generally it is toxins that cause free radicals—toxins from food, drugs, pollution, chemicals, etc. Antioxidants have the ability to neutralize free radicals and render them harmless, after which the body will eliminate them.

Blueberries also provide substantial amounts of vitamins B1, B2, C, and E, manganese, and dietary fiber. They are known to be heart-healthy and are also good for visual, brain, gastrointestinal, and colon health.

Brazil Nuts

Brazil nuts *(Bertholletia excelsa)* come from a large broad-leafed evergreen tree. These enormous trees can reach heights of 150 feet or more. Growing in the Amazon rain forests of South America, they can live 500 to 800 years. They don't start producing nuts until the trees are about twenty years old. There are a few plantations in Brazil, but most harvests are gathered from wild trees. Clusters of Brazil nuts, each in their own shell, grow inside a coconut-like fruit pod found at the end of branches.

Brazil nuts are most famous for being the highest food source of selenium, a powerful antioxidant proven to protect against heart disease and prostate cancer. Selenium stimulates the immune system and discourages the ageing process. Brazil nuts are also loaded with other nutrients such as zinc, magnesium, thiamine, phosphorus, copper, and iron. It is a very fatty nut, with the fat content breaking down to 25% saturated fat (medium-chain), 41% monounsaturated fat, and 34% polyunsaturated fat.

Butternut Squash

One of many winter-harvest squash varieties, butternut squash *(Cucurbita moschata)* is a member of the gourd family. It is bottle-shaped and light orange in color. Ideally the inside flesh is bright orange and quite sweet in flavor. Choose squash that have a hard, deep-colored rind free of blemishes or moldy spots. If possible, try to see what color the inside is. You only want to use raw squash if it is perfectly ripe; otherwise there just isn't enough flavor and it can be hard to digest. Butternut squash is a great source of vitamins A and C, and also contains significant quantities of potassium, iron, magnesium, and beta-carotene.

Cashews

Cashews *(Anacardium occidentale)* are in the same family as poison oak, ivy, and sumac, along with mango and pistachio. Like the others in this family, the cashew tree contains powerful chemical irritants. These irritants are found in the shell oil but not in the nuts themselves. However, there is also some irritant toxin residue on the inside of the shell layer. If the shell is not opened correctly, this residue will get on the cashew nut, making it inedible. Cooking the cashews deactivates the toxin, which is why most suppliers steam the shell open at high temperatures, thus cooking the nut inside. These nuts, though, are often sold as "raw" simply because they were not roasted. This is why cashews are usually seen roasted and never sold in the shell.

SunFood Nutrition is a reliable, truly raw cashew source. Truly raw cashews are much sweeter, tastier, and nutritious than regular cashews. Truly raw cashews are rich in potassium, magnesium, calcium, vitamins B1, B2, B6, and E, niacin, and folate.

Cherries

Cherries come from a large tree that has been cultivated around the world since prehistoric times. The cherry tree *(Prunus avium)* belongs to a large family of fruit trees that includes apricot, apple, plum, and peach. Cherries come in three main categories: sweet, sour, and wild. Sweet cherries are the most commonly consumed, while sour cherries are most often cooked and used for preserves, jams, and liqueurs.

Rich in many nutrients, cherries are most noted for their high antioxidant content and also as one of the best food sources of iron. Interestingly, cherries contain more melatonin than any other fruit. Melatonin is a type of tryptamine (brain chemical) that is naturally produced in our brains, but certain foods contain or can stimulate production of this chemical (see Chapter 7, the section titled "Benefits of Raw Cacao"). Melatonin is known to be relaxing and sleep-inducing.

Cinnamon

Cinnamon *(Cinnamomum zeylanicum)*, one of the oldest spices known, comes from the bark of a small evergreen tree native to Sri Lanka (Ceylon). The related species *Cassia (Cinnamomum aromatica)* is usually what is sold as "cinnamon" in stores. Both species are wonderful, aromatic spices used worldwide in savory and sweet foods. True cinnamon, usually called Ceylon cinnamon, is sweeter and less potent than cassia, with more subtle aromatic nuances. It is harder to find and more expensive. There are several other cinnamon varieties which all possess a similar aromatic bark.

Cinnamon is very helpful for treating diarrhea and other digestive problems. It is extremely high in antioxidants and has antimicrobial properties. Cinnamon is especially known for its ability to normalize blood sugar levels, making it very helpful for diabetics. Cinnamon is high in the trace mineral manganese and also contains iron and calcium. Cinnamon will lose its freshness fairly quickly (like any powdered spice), usually after six months. If it doesn't smell sweet, discard and get some new.

Citrus (Lemons, Limes, and Oranges)

Lemons *(Citrus limon)* and limes *(Citrus latifolia)* contain unique flavonoid compounds that have antioxidant and anti-cancer properties. Lemons/limes are an excellent source of one of the most important antioxidants in nature, vitamin C, the primary water-soluble antioxidant in the body. It travels through the body, neutralizing any free radicals with which it comes into contact (inside *and* outside cells). Vitamin C is also vital to the functioning of a strong immune system.

Citrus Mandala

Despite the obvious acidity of these fruits, they actually have an alkaline effect in the body. There are many different varieties of lemons and limes, and the best citrus always seem to come from someone's backyard. Yummy exotic varieties abound like Meyer lemons, which are very sweet and floral, and Key limes, which are very bitter but with an amazing aromatic essence. When selecting citrus, look for smooth skins with a strong aroma.

Oranges *(Citrus sinensis)* are probably the most widely consumed of all the citrus fruits. The orange is native to China and has been cultivated in Asia for more than four thousand years. Today the orange is one of the most important commercial fruit crops in the world. Oranges are classified as either bitter or sweet; sweet oranges come in many different varieties such as Valencia, Navel, and the delicious Blood Orange. Oranges are known for their high concentration of vitamin C, and they are also a good source of potassium. Choose oranges that are firm, smooth, heavy for their size, and have no soft or dark spots.

Clove

The clove is a delicious aromatic spice, aptly described in its botanical name, *Eugenia aromaticum.* They are the dried flower buds of a tree native to Indonesia. This omnipresent spice is commercially cultivated mainly in Zanzibar, Indonesia, and Madagascar. Cloves are used whole or ground up in savory and sweet dishes. It is a major spice in Indian cooking, particularly in North India, where it is used in almost every sauce and side dish made. Cloves are used in chai (spiced tea), are smoked in a type of cigarette popular in Indonesia, and are an ingredient in Chinese and Japanese incense.

Cloves are utilized in Ayurvedic and Chinese traditional medicines as well as Western herbalism and dentistry, where the essential oil is used as a numbing agent. This distinctive spice is also considered beneficial for the stomach and digestion.

Cloves, like any spice, actually have a shelf life. Many people hang on to herbs that are decades old, when really all that flavor is long gone. Pungent spices such as clove may lose their real flair within a year. Really fresh cloves are truly amazing and have an extremely powerful aroma. We recommend buying just as much clove as you need, and whole so you can grind them at home with a coffee grinder. Clove is an indispensable flavor, along with its best friends cinnamon and nutmeg, in many dishes such as pumpkin pie. It should be used sparingly since the intense flavor can easily become overwhelming. As with its use in food, too much clove used medicinally can have several toxic side effects. Basically, it is a powerful spice to respect the power of.

Coconut

The coconut *(Cocos nucifera)* is often referred to as the "tree of life," for it can provide pretty much everything one needs (in the tropics, at least). You can eat the coconut flesh and drink the water, build shelter from the leaf fronds alone, make a sturdy boat or raft, fashion bowls, knives, spoons, etc., from the coconut shell, make clothing from the husk, and the list goes on and on.

Humans and the coconut tree have a very closely linked connection. In Hawaii the traditional natives will plant a coconut tree when a baby is born. This tree will provide for the newborn their whole life, since the average life span of a coconut tree is eighty to ninety years. Other interesting connections: a coconut tree reaches sexual maturity (starts to fruit) around the age of twelve to thirteen; and the coconut seed (technically classified as a seed though often thought of as a fruit, or even more erroneously, a nut) takes nine months to develop from a flower to being ripe and ready for harvest (or to fall to the ground).

It is generally agreed that coconut water is the most pure form of water on Earth. The water in the coconut is slowly filtered through the whole tree for nine months. Coconut water contains nature's perfect electrolyte balance, as well as enzymes and vitamins. The water is extremely similar to human blood—it is virtually identical to the plasma, which, combined with hemoglobin (red blood cells), is blood. During the Pearl Harbor (Hawaii) crisis, coconut water was directly transfused into wounded people due to lack of blood. It seems that humans and the coconut are in many ways cosmically linked.

Raw coconut oil is made from cold-pressed mature coconut meat. Coconut oil when cold is white and solid, melting into clear oil at 78°. Coconut oil is a raw saturated fat containing mostly medium-chain fatty acids, which the body can metabolize efficiently and convert to energy quickly. By weight, coconut oil has less calories than any other fat source. Coconut oil contains absolutely no cholesterol and actually helps to balance cholesterol levels. Recently coconut oil received recognition by many health professionals and has even been dubbed the "diet fat" because it helps the body to break up accumulated fats in the system and metabolize them. This oil contains the second-highest amount of lauric acid (which is anti-viral and anti-microbial) found in any source; only mother's milk has more.

Another amazing product from the coconut palm is coconut sugar, made by collecting the nectar that drips from the cut flower stalks, and boiling and filtering it until a crystallized sugar develops. Extensively used in India, Thailand, and other southeast Asian countries, this sugar is actually low-glycemic! It is also extremely delicious, and although it isn't raw, it is much more nutritious than cane sugar and a fantastic alternative.

Dates

The date tree *(Phoenix dactylifera)* is a type of palm that has been extensively cultivated throughout history for its edible fruit. It is believed to have originated in the desert oases of northern Africa and also southwest Asia. Date trees can grow quite tall and large and stay in production for more than sixty years. The dates grow in clusters below the fronds and can number between six hundred and seventeen hundred dates per cluster.

Dates are loaded with energy. They're high in dietary fiber and carbohydrates, and contain more potassium than bananas. They are also high in many of the B vitamins, magnesium, and iron. Iron is essential to red blood cell production, and red blood cells carry all the nutrients to cells throughout the body.

There are many different kinds of dates, all with varying flavor and texture nuances, as well as different levels of sweetness. Medjool dates are the most popular and easily accessible variety, and they also happen to be the sweetest. Other delicious varieties include Khadrawy, Halawi, and Thoory dates. We certainly don't recommend using the date "pellets" one finds in stores sometimes, which are coated in flour, sugar, or corn starch. Date paste is called for in many of our raw desserts, and it is easily made (see Chapter 1); yet it is sold commercially from only a select number of places. Dates store very well in an airtight container in or out of the fridge.

Flax Seeds

Flax seeds (from the species *Linum usitatissimum*) are very rich in nutrients, especially essential fatty acids (EFAs) and soluble fiber. Flax seeds have a balanced ratio of EFAs including omega-3, omega-6, and omega-9 fatty acids. When moistened, flax seeds are very mucilaginous. They are easy on the digestive system and act as a gentle laxative.

Ginger

Ginger *(Zingiber officinale)* is a knotted, thick, beige, underground stem (rhizome). Originating in southern China, cultivation of this popular spice has spread to India, southeast Asia, west Africa, the Caribbean, and Hawaii. Ginger thrives best in the tropics or warmer temperate regions. There are dozens of varieties other than the one kind used as food. Many varieties are not edible but produce gorgeous flowers in all different colors, shapes, and sizes.

Ginger has been used and recognized throughout history as a medicinal herb. The Chinese have been using ginger to aid digestion and treat upset stomach and diarrhea for at least two thousand years. Ginger possesses certain phytonutrients that are powerful anti-inflammatory compounds (gingerols and shogaols). Ginger has warming properties that help to get the blood moving and relieve congestion and soreness, due to its property that affects microcirculation in the body.

Goji Berries

Goji berries *(Lycium barbarum)* are generally considered one of the most nutrient-rich foods available. They are the bright red fruit of a smallish tree that grows mainly in Asia. Goji berries have a three-thousand-year history in traditional Chinese medicine. The Chinese have been cultivating this alkaline fruit for thousands of years and even hold an annual two-week festival in its honor.

Goji berries contain eighteen amino acids and twenty-one minerals, including germanium, an anti-cancer trace mineral rarely found in foods. They contain about 13% protein, which is more than whole wheat. They are the richest food source of antioxidant carotenoids including beta-carotene and zeaxanthin, and are also rich in phytonutients, especially beta-sitosterol, an anti-inflammatory agent known to lower cholesterol and treat impotence. Other identified phytonutrients contained in goji berries include betaine, physalin, solavetivone, and cyperone.

Choose goji berries that are bright in color and show no dark spots.

Hempseeds

The hemp plant *(Cannabis ruderalis)* has been used for thousands of years all over the world. It is believed to have originated in China, and the great Chinese Emperor Shen-Nung promoted hemp as one of the "elixirs of immortality" all the way back in 2300 BC. The hemp plant is grown for fuel, food, and fiber and is the botanical cousin to marijuana. Hemp does not contain THC, the intoxicating chemical found in marijuana. The seed of the hemp plant is particularly nutritious. It is a unique complete protein in that 65% of that protein is what's called "globulin edestin," which makes hempseed the highest known source of this protein in the plant kingdom. This type of protein closely resembles human blood plasma and is highly compatible with it, meaning it is easily absorbed, digested, and utilized by the body. Hempseed is packed with antioxidants and contains a balanced ratio of essential fatty acids (EFAs), including linoleic, alpha-linolenic, gamma-linolenic (GLA), and stearidonic (SDA) acids. All of these EFAs are crucial for good health. GLA is a special omega-6 fatty acid found in algae and hempseeds that helps the body reduce inflammation.

Choose hempseeds that have been shelled to ensure they are raw; hempseeds found in the shell have usually been heated somehow so they cannot germinate and grow.

Lavender

Lavender *(Lavandula angustifolia)* is part of a genus of about thirty species of flowering plants in the mint family. This plant is native to the Mediterranean region, south to tropical Africa and the southwest regions of India. The most common variety is *Lavandula angustifolia* (formerly known as *Lavandula officinalis*), native to the Western Mediterranean regions, primarily in the Pyrenees and other mountains of northern Spain. It is a strongly aromatic flowering shrub that grows three to six feet with evergreen leaves and pinkish-purple flowers. The flowers and leaves have long been used as an herbal medicine, either in the form of oil or as an herbal tea. Flowers are also used as a culinary herb, most often as a part of the French blend "herbes de Provence," or they can be candied and used for cake decorations. Lavender oil is used as an antiseptic and in aromatherapy. Because of its ability to induce relaxation, the oil has many applications in massage therapy, lotions, eye pillows, bath oils, balms, salves, etc. Lavender infusion is claimed to soothe and heal insect bites, and to soothe headaches. It also frequently used to promote good relaxed sleep and for the treatment of skin burns and inflammatory conditions.

Maca

Maca root *(Lepidium peruvianum)* comes from a perennial plant that grows between 13,000 and 15,000 feet above sea level in the high Andean plateaus of Peru. Maca's tuberous root resembles those of its relatives, the radish. The native Peruvians have used this superfood for its nourishing as well as medicinal properties since the days of the Incas. The dry maca powder, with its sweet and mild spicy flavor, is still considered a delicacy and is widely used by the Peruvians.

Scientific studies are gradually confirming the effect attributed to this plant, which has long been used to enhance health; increase energy, endurance, and stamina; to help treat symptoms of menopause and regulate menstrual cycles; to stimulate brain functions and aid the endocrine system; and as a natural aphrodisiac. Because maca is an adaptogen, it works with your body's metabolism to repair what needs to be repaired so that an ideal level of energy is maintained at all times. Maca contains four alkaloids that have proven to nourish the body's endocrine's glands and the glandular functions, promoting hormonal balance and aiding the reproductive system in both women and men. It's rich in calcium, magnesium, and iron and contains trace minerals such as zinc, iodine, selenium, copper, and manganese as well as B vitamins. Maca is a real gift from the Earth!

Macadamias

Macadamias *(Macadamia integrifolia)* come from a large tree that likes to grow in rainforests and other moist, frost-free climates. A macadamia tree will start producing nuts at about seven years and may produce in ever-increasing numbers for over a century. Most macadamias are exported from Hawaii, Australia, South Africa, and Central America.

The nuts are the creamy white kernel inside a hard, thick shell, which is inside an even thicker, dense husk. It is a process to get the nut out, and this definitely accounts for part of macadamias' high price. Macadamias (mac nuts) are the fattiest nut, containing up to 80% fat. This high oil content is what makes mac nuts so delicious and nutritious, but it also makes them very sensitive to light, air, and temperature—meaning they spoil easily. Keep mac nuts refrigerated or frozen for the longer term. An especially yellowish color indicates that the nut has gone rancid.

All that fat is mostly monounsaturated fat. Mac nuts are the highest plant source of monounsaturated fat, as well as omega-9 and omega-7 fatty acids. Omega-9 fatty acid (oleic acid) is very useful in reducing "bad" cholesterol and increasing HDL cholesterol production (the good cholesterol). Macadamia oil is prized for containing 22% omega-7 fatty acid (palmitoleic acid), which makes it a vegan alternative to mink oil (which contains 17%). Palmitoleic acid is used in many cosmetics and skincare products. Omega-7 and -9 fatty acids are generally considered hydrating and healing for the skin.

In addition, mac nuts are the second-highest plant source of selenium (Brazil nuts are number one). Selenium builds selenium superoxide dismutase, which is the body's most potent antioxidant enzyme. Mac nuts also contain vitamins A, B1, B2, niacin, calcium, iron, and zinc.

Mint

The Mentha or mint family of herbs includes twenty-five species and many hybrids thereof, but the most commonly used varieties are spearmint *(Mentha spicata)* and peppermint. Other delicious and exotic varieties include gingermint, applemint, pineapple mint, and chocolate mint. The mint family has been cultivated and used medicinally for a very long time, and the plants are highly revered for their wonderful cooling flavor. Mentha plants are extremely aromatic perennial herbs, known for their therapeutic properties in holistically treating stomach, chest, lung, and digestive problems. Peppermint contains more oil than spearmint and is generally considered to be of more medicinal value. Spearmint is mainly a culinary herb and is the type of mint we mostly use in our recipes.

Mulberries

Mulberries *(Morus alba)* are the fruit of a tree native to Africa, Asia, and the Americas. Traditionally, mulberry fruit has been used as a medicinal agent to treat afflictions of the blood and kidneys. It is also used to treat weakness, fatigue, and anemia. It is useful during or after a long illness as a restorative and is known to be alkalizing to the system. Mulberries contain a significant amount of resveratol (a phytoalexin). Studies have shown resveratol to have anti-cancer, antiviral, neuroprotective, and anti-inflammatory effects. Mulberries are rich in vitamin A, potassium, phosphorus, and calcium. They are a good source of dietary fiber, riboflavin, and magnesium, as well as vitamin C, vitamin K, and iron.

Nutmeg

Nutmeg *(Myristica fragrans)* is a wonderful spice used extensively both in desserts and savory cuisine. It is the seed of the nutmeg tree, an evergreen native to the Molluccas or Spice Islands of Indonesia. It grows in most tropical climates but is mainly cultivated in Indonesia, India, Sri Lanka, and the West Indies. The trees grow to a height of about thirty feet with oblong dark green leaves about four inches long.

The nutmeg fruit resembles an apricot—golden yellow with red spots. When the fruit is ripe, its flesh splits open to reveal a brown kernel (the nutmeg) about an inch long, which is covered by a bright red membrane (mace). Nutmeg and mace have similar taste qualities: nutmeg has generally a warm spicy and sweet flavor, while mace is more delicate in flavor and gives off an aroma similar to cinnamon.

Nutmeg helps to aid digestion, reduce flatulence, and is a source of minerals such as potassium, phosphorus, calcium, magnesium, and iron. It also contains myristin, which is a narcotic substance with euphoric properties. It's a powerful spice, and too much of it can lead to headaches and stomachaches.

Since nutmeg quickly loses its flavor when ground, the best way to use it is to buy whole kernels and grate it as needed. When you buy the kernels be sure to check them for insect holes and to choose the hard and heavy ones. You can also poke the nutmeg with a needle: you should see a drop or an oily film rise to the surface, which indicates a fresh kernel. Nutmeg is an essential spice to have in the creation of most fall/winter desserts, is a "must" for the year-round carrot cake, and makes a nice addition to many other dishes.

Pears

This is a truly ancient fruit. The pear tree *(Pyrus communis)* is native to the northern region of Asia and is believed to have been consumed even in prehistoric times. Highly esteemed by ancient Greeks, Romans, Egyptians, and Chinese, this fruit has been cultivated for at least three thousand years. Today's variety is the result of hybridizations carried out during the seventeenth and eighteenth centuries. Pears are related to apples, almonds, and apricots, and like their family members they grow well in temperate zones, though pears are slightly more sensitive to temperature variations. Today's largest pear production countries are China, Italy, the United States, and Russia.

Some varieties have an almost perfectly round shape, while most pears have a distinct teardrop shape. The skin is usually really soft and thin and may be yellow, brown, red, or green. Pears can greatly vary in texture and flavor, depending on the variety and time of harvesting, but they are usually finely textured and juicy. Harvesting time can range from summer to winter in warmer regions. The most cultivated varieties are the Anjou, Passe-Crassane, and Comice from France; Bartlett and Conference from England; Packham from Australia; Bosh from Belgium; and Rocha from Portugal.

Pears contain potassium and sodium and are rich in fiber. Dry pears have a much higher nutrient content, making this fruit ideal for dehydration. Dry pears are rich in potassium, are a good source of copper and iron, and contain magnesium, vitamin C, phosphorus, and sodium.

Always choose ripe pears that are smooth and firm but not overly hard. Unripe pears are difficult to digest. Simply leave the pear out at room temperature until ripe. Once ripe, they should be eaten really soon or kept in the fridge for a few days.

Pecans

Pecans *(Carya illinoinensis)* originated in the Mississippi River valley of North America. These giant trees can live anywhere from 100 to 1,000 years, and one tree can produce more than 400 pounds of nuts in one year. The flavor of pecans is sweeter and more delicate than walnuts, with a distinct butter-like taste due to the high oil content.

Pecans are known to help correct cholesterol imbalances and to lower the risk of gallstone and heart disease. Pecans contain more than nineteen vitamins and minerals as well as phytonutrients—they are high in zinc, vitamins A and E, folic acid, calcium, magnesium, phosphorus, potassium, and several of the B vitamins. Pecans are 60% monounsaturated fat, 30% polyunsaturated fat, and 10% saturated fat (medium-chain fatty acid).

Persimmons

The persimmon tree belongs to the family of hardwoods that includes ebony and is the only tree within this family to bear edible fruit. A native of China and southeast Europe, persimmon is now widely cultivated in Brazil, Korea, Israel, the United States, and Japan (where it is also the national fruit known as "kaki"). It was known to the ancient Greeks as "the wheat of Zeus" or "fruit of the gods."

There are two main groups of persimmons which include hundreds of varieties: the Asian persimmon *(Diospyros kaki)*, which has been known and cultivated for thousands of years, and the American persimmon *(Diospyros virginiana)*, which grows wild in the southeastern United Sates. American Indians were known to dry persimmons, making this fruit available year-round.

The Hachiya and the Fuyu are the most common cultivated varieties within the Asian group. The Hachiya persimmon is heart-shaped and has a bright red-orange skin and flesh. This kind of persimmon should always be consumed when it is soft and fully ripe, as its high tannin content makes it very astringent and inedible if consumed before maturation. Ripe persimmons taste fragrant and very sweet, slightly viscous with an almost liquid texture. The Fuyu persimmon contains no tannins and can be consumed when the fruit is still firm. Persimmons will ripen at room temperature, and if you wish to hasten this process simply place them in a paper bag with an apple or banana.

Persimmons are a good source of vitamin A, potassium, vitamin C, and copper, and they provide a mild laxative effect.

Pineapple

The pineapple *(Ananas comosus)* belongs to the large Bromeliaceae family and is the only plant in this family to bear edible fruit. Pineapples are cultivated in most tropical regions and are believed to have originated in Brazil. The fruit grows on a herbaceous perennial plant, which attains a height of about three feet. The plant produces a hundred or more purple flowers that grow in a spiral pattern around a central axis. These unfertilized flowers join together to form a single fruit, the pineapple, which then takes eighteen to twenty months to mature into the large fruit, which can weigh between four and nine pounds.

Pineapples are high in vitamin C and also contain large amounts of the anti-inflammatory enzyme bromelain. Numerous varieties are produced commercially, the most common being Cayenne, Queen, Red Spanish, and Pernambuco. Choose pineapples that aren't too soft, have a strong aroma, and no dark spots.

Pistachios

Pistachios *(Pistacia vera)* are the seeds of a deciduous tree native to Asia Minor. They grow wild in the mountainous regions of central Asia and are highly cultivated in that area, as well as the Mediterranean region of Europe and now in California. Pistachios grow in clusters and are harvested by hand or by a machine, which shakes the nuts to the ground where they are gathered. This hardy tree is more drought-resistant than any other fruit tree and is also extremely frost-resistant. In its natural habitat the pistachio tree can exceed a life span of a hundred and fifty years. Pistachio nuts have a very specific flavor, slightly sweet and with a spice-like quality. They are 83% unsaturated fat (consisting of 68% monounsaturated and 15% polyunsaturated). They are an excellent source of potassium, magnesium, copper, thiamine and are also rich in iron, phosphorus, folic acid, vitamins C and B6, zinc, and dietary fiber.

Store pistachios in an airtight container in the fridge for maximum freshness.

Pomegranate

The name of this fruit comes from the Latin *granatum* which means "fruit of many seeds." The pomegranate tree *(Punica granatum)* is a native of Persia, where it was cultivated at least four thousand years ago. It has been widely used in ancient Egypt, Mesopotamia, and China as well as throughout Europe, and it still plays an important role in Iranian cooking today. The tree grows in most tropical and subtropical climates with hot summers and cold winters. Today the main producers of pomegranate are Iran, India, and the United States.

Pomegranate trees can grow to a height of twenty to twenty-four feet and produce large trumpet-shaped flowers. The fruits are generally harvested five to seven months after flowering, when they are fully mature. Once picked from the tree the fruit does not continue ripening. The pomegranate has a thick and leather-like skin that is not edible. The inside of the fruit is divided in six parts by a thick white membrane, and each section contains edible seeds. Pomegranate seeds can be crimson red, pink, or pinkish, depending on the variety. The seeds are very juicy and pleasantly refreshing with a tangy-sweet flavor. The characteristic tart flavor in pomegranate results from the high content of numerous organic acids, including high citric acid. The fruit is a good source of potassium and vitamin C, and also has traces of sodium and niacin. Pomegranate contains many phytochemicals with antioxidant and anti-carcinogenic properties such as ellagic acid.

When buying pomegranate avoid wrinkled fruit and those with dull and pale skin. The freshest and best pomegranates should have a bright-colored skin with tinges of brown. Pomegranates can be left out at room temperature for a few days and will store well in the fridge for up to three weeks.

Soy Lecithin

Soy lecithin (less-ih-thin) consists of three types of phospholipids, which are phosphorus-rich oils. It is extracted from soybean oil and generally used as a natural emulsifier in various food applications. Lecithin is an excellent source of choline, which is essential to every living cell in the body and is one of the main components in cell membranes. Without choline, the cell membranes would harden, prohibiting important nutrients from entering and leaving the cell. Scientists believe that lecithin and choline may aid in memory and cognitive function, cardiovascular health, and liver function. Lecithin protects cells from oxidation and largely comprises the protective sheaths surrounding the brain. In fact, about 30% of the brain's dry weight is lecithin! The body's own lecithin is continually being produced by the liver. The body needs lecithin for proper brain and nervous system functioning. Unless the liver is impaired in some way, it is not necessary to take supplemental lecithin.

In raw dessert making, lecithin is not always used (mainly because it's not raw), and when it is, usually only a small amount is sufficient since it does not take much to achieve the emulsifying effect. The purpose of using soy lecithin in raw desserts is to emulsify and homogenize the fat and the liquid so they don't separate, and it also helps make the desserts creamier.

This ingredient usually needs to be mail-ordered from a reliable source (please see resource section at end of Chapter 1). Soy lecithin is highly susceptible to rancidity, meaning it is sensitive to light and temperature. Most available soy lecithin is old and rancid, not to mention non-organic and genetically modified. Any lecithin that is a bright, vibrant yellow color has gone rancid—good lecithin should be a light beige color. To safely store it, keep in an airtight container in the fridge.

If you have an aversion or allergy to soy, any of the recipes can be made without the lecithin; they just won't come out exactly the same. Simply omit the lecithin from the recipe, blend a little longer than usual, and add a couple extra tablespoons of coconut oil.

Strawberries

Strawberries *(Fragaria xananassa)* are the most versatile and widely used berry in desserts. Their rich red color and juicy sweet flavor make these fruits an all-time favorite in many recipes. It is the fruit of the strawberry plant, a perennial that grows all over the world in temperate zones. Some varieties of strawberry come from Europe while others are native to South and North America. There are more than six hundred different varieties of strawberries today, and they all differ in size, color, texture, and flavor. The first crossing of two wild varieties (the ancestors of today's commercial strawberry) was successfully done in 1714 by François Amédée Frézier (a Frenchman).

The strawberry plant is a low-growing shrub that produces horizontal runners from its base, which take root to produce new plants. The strawberries themselves are not really fruits. Officially, in the botanical sense of term, the fruit part of the strawberry is the yellowish seed that dots the berry's surface. What we eat and consider the fruit is in fact the result of the swelling of the plant's stalk.

Strawberries have many health benefits. They are an incredible source of vitamin C, potassium, folic acid, vitamin B5, and magnesium. They also have tonic, detoxifying, diuretic, re-mineralizing, and astringent properties. Strawberry essence is used commercially in beauty products for the prevention of wrinkles and freckles and as an overall skin tonic. Eaten in large quantities, strawberry will act as a laxative. Whole strawberries contain higher nutritional value than chopped strawberries (particularly vitamin C) since less surface is exposed to the air (oxidization). The best way to reduce vitamin C loss in cut strawberries is to add lemon juice or apple juice to them. They are very perishable and really need to be stored in the fridge as soon as possible. Wash strawberries right before using them and without hulling them (cutting off the green part) to prevent losing their juice. As with all berries, they should just be rinsed and never soaked in water.

Always choose carefully the strawberries you want to buy. Choose firm berries with a healthy bright color, and check the bottom of the container to make sure all the berries are in good condition.

Sugarcane

The infamous sugarcane *(Saccharum officinarum)* is a variety of tall perennial grasses (of the botanical family Poaceae) and is native to warm temperate and tropical climates. These grasses have thick, fibrous stalks that can easily reach heights exceeding ten feet. Juice is pressed out of the stalks and turned into some form of sugar.

About two hundred countries grow this crop, producing roughly 1,350 million tons of sugar annually, with the world's largest producer being Brazil. That's a lot of sugar, but it is the second most abundantly traded world commodity (oil being first).

There are many uses for the crop other than edible sugar, such as making rum, cachaça (the national spirit of Brazil), and ethanol for fuel. The processing of regular white sugar is ridiculously complex and toxic, including chemical solutions, bleaching, and endless filtering with things like activated carbon and bone charcoal ("bone char" is the reason some white sugars are not vegan). These procedures are extreme and not good at all for the environment; the only really "green" thing being done with sugarcane is its use in ethanol production.

Everyone pretty much knows at this point that white sugar is not healthy. Some people will say it is the worst (edible) food possible to put in your body. There is a lot of information about the negative effects of sugar, but there are alternatives! So many other choices exist in the realm of natural sweeteners such as agave syrup, honey, yacon syrup, stevia, date sugar, maple sugar, coconut sugar, brown rice syrup, barley malt, and xylitol (which is a practically non-glycemic sugar crystal extracted from either birch or corn). We promote the use of these more natural, nutrient-rich, and easier-on-the-Earth sweeteners for most of the food we make. However for the raw chocolate items, we use sucanat as part of the sweetener, which works very well. Sucanat (sugar cane natural) is sugar in its most natural form. The freshly squeezed cane juice is simply evaporated with low heat, so essentially only the water is removed. This basic and non-invasive method produces a slightly coarse, matte, tan-colored sugar. It has a good flavor yet it is subtle. Cane juice and sucanat are a good source of riboflavin (vitamin B2) and a handful of other minerals including calcium, copper, and manganese. Sucanat is usually organically grown, non-GMO, fair trade, and raw!

Turmeric

Turmeric *(Curcuma longa)* is a pungent root from the ginger family. This is a very medicinal food, often used in Ayurvedic remedies. Most people know turmeric in its powdered bright-yellow form, but before processing it is a root that looks like ginger, only smaller and more profusely branched. Fresh is really best (for savory dishes), but for desserts the powder works better, and it is only used as a coloring agent. Use only one-eighth of a teaspoon or less in desserts so you don't taste the turmeric too much (know that the flavor and color develop over time). Turmeric has strong anti-inflammatory, antioxidant, anti-microbial, and anti-cancer properties. It contains the phytonutrient curcumin, which has been proven to fight cancer and is a potent anti-inflammatory agent. Turmeric is also a great blood purifier, which makes it extremely beneficial for skin health.

Vanilla

Vanilla pods (or "beans") are actually from an orchid called *Vanilla planifolia* which is the only type of orchid out of the 35,000 known varieties to produce edible fruit. These fruits are seven- to eight-inch-long, green bean-looking pods which are picked green and then need to dry and ferment to develop that rich vanilla flavor. It is a complicated process taking many months, which is why the price is so high.

Vanilla has an aphrodisiac type of magic. Vanilla's energy is female, which naturally combines well with cacao, which has male energy. In plant mythologies, Vanilla and Cacao were divine lovers who eventually took plant form. Since vanilla is a breatharian orchid, it will sometimes even grow in a cacao tree!

When buying vanilla beans, look for full-length beans six to eight inches long. The best varieties will be labeled Madagascar, Tahitian, or Mexican vanilla beans. The beans should be plump, supple, moist, glossy, and have a rich aroma. Avoid dry, woody, short, and scentless beans. Vanilla beans will store indefinitely in an airtight container placed in a cool, dark place. Don't refrigerate beans as this can cause them to harden and possibly take on refrigerator smell.

Some beans may develop a frosting of natural vanillin crystals if you keep them for a while. Called "givre" in French (which means "light frost"), these crystals indicate that the beans are high in natural vanillin and are of very good quality. However, mildew can also give the same appearance. If you are unsure if it is mildew or vanillin crystals, you should be able to identify the mildew by the smell (also, the vanillin crystals will sparkle in the sunlight whereas mildew will not).

Walnuts

The walnut tree *(Juglans regia)* originated in northern India and on the shores of the Caspian Sea where it has been cultivated for thousands of years. It was first introduced into Europe by the Romans in the fourth century and regarded as a sacred tree by both Romans and Greeks because of its longevity.

Today the leading producers of walnuts are the United States, Turkey, China, Romania, Iran, France, and the Balkan countries. Many parts of the tree along with the nourishing nut have long been used in a variety of ways. The edible oil extracted from nuts was used to provide light; the leaves and walnuts were consumed for their medicinal properties; the husk was used and still is to make liqueurs and flavored wines; and the shell was used to make a dye. The numerous species of walnut include the black walnut, the white or butternut walnut, and the renowned-worldwide French variety known as "noix de Grenoble" from the Grenoble region.

The walnut shell is covered with a smooth, sticky green husk known as the "shuck," and the two kernels are joined together with small portions separated by membranes. The walnut kernels are off-white in color and covered with a thin layer of light to dark yellow skin. Walnuts contain up to 86% unsaturated fat, and their high content of omega-3s and antioxidants makes them unique among tree nuts. Walnuts are an excellent source of copper and magnesium, and a good source of potassium, vitamin B6, carotenoids and melatonin. They also contain phosphorus, niacin, and iron. Walnuts are a great source of vitamins A and E, along with alpha-linoleic acid, a major heart-healthy acid. Walnuts also contain ellagic acid, an anticarcinogen and antioxidant also found in pomegranates. To best preserve them, keep walnuts protected from humidity, heat, air, and light.

Yacon Syrup

Yacon *(Smallanthus sonchifolius)* is a type of plant native to Peru, where it grows in the high altitudes of the Andes. It is the root of a tall, leafy plant that produces tiny yellow sunflowers. Yacon root contains a special type of sugar known as oligofructose, or fructo-oligosaccharide (FOS). The human body has no enzyme to hydrolyze (process) FOS. This means it is not converted to glucose in the bloodstream and thus passes through the digestive tract unmetabolized. These unmetabolized sugars then become food for the "friendly" bacteria that live in the colon, increasing their population and simultaneously decreasing harmful bacteria. When something has this effect on our intestinal flora it is known as a "prebiotic" and is very beneficial for overall colon health. It regulates intestinal flora, which reduces constipation; improves absorption of calcium, magnesium, and other vitamins; reduces cholesterol and triglyceride levels; and boosts the immune system. Since the body cannot process the FOS type of sugar, it is generally referred to as "sugar-free" and is not on the glycemic index.

This makes yacon an ideal sweetener for diabetics and other people with sugar sensitivities. It is also low in calories, containing half the calories of honey. The syrup of the root is what is mainly used, and it resembles molasses in color, consistency, and flavor. The flavor is delicious, malty, and has a faint cinnamon-like spice to it.

Index

About the Authors

Tiziana Alipo Tamborra

Tiziana Alipo Tamborra brings a wide range of skills and experience to her current practice as a dessert chef. Her passion for desserts is a lifelong journey she started in Italy, inspired by her mother and grandmother. In the early nineties she started to study macrobiotic  philosophy and began to develop her own recipes for vegan, macrobiotic desserts. Alipo Tamborra came to California in 1997 to continue her studies and has since been involved in health and nutrition, baked for several International Macrobiotic Conferences and cruises, and managed two vegan bakeries. She has worked as a private chef and pastry chef, and taught cooking classes since 1998 in Italy, Canada, and the U.S. Her holistic approach to health includes acupressure training and Somatic Experiencing. Alipo Tamborra is currently the bakery manager at Café Gratitude and has been with the company since 2005. She lives in Oakland, California, with her husband, Henry, and their cat, Scooby.

Matthew Rogers

Matthew Rogers is a longtime food and nutrition enthusiast. Having trained as a pastry chef, he soon thereafter explored the world of vegan and raw-food preparation. For several years he lived and worked on an organic permaculture farm in Maui, where he learned many of the secrets and benefits of organic, raw foods. Rogers joined the Café Gratitude team shortly after its inception in 2004. Since then he has mastered the making of raw desserts for the company and has been teaching raw dessert classes since 2006. He is especially fascinated with the nutritional  and healing values of raw food and strives to raise this awareness in others. Rogers lives in San Francisco, California.